REAL GUIDE – TO GENERATING MULTIPLE STREAMS OF INCOME

First Edition: October 2014
ISBN Numbers:

E-Book: 978-981-09-2635-9
Digitized Book: 978-981-09-2636-6
Hardback/ Hardcover: 978-981-09-2633-5
Paperback/Softcover: 978-981-09-2634-2

For permissions requests, contact:
Raj Singh and Vanpeak Pte Ltd. (Singapore)
71 Ubi Crescent, Excalibur Center, #04-11, Singapore 408571
Phone: +65 62640889
Website: www.vanpeak.com

CONTENTS

CHAPTER ONE:

MULTIPLE INCOME STREAMS AND PASSIVE INCOME

In 1964, an investor purchased controlling stock shares in a failing textile company. This investor had an idea of using the income generated from the ownership of this company to fund the purchasing of stock in other companies. However, the owner would only be actively involved in the management of the first company. The income streams from the other companies would be passive income.

This investor was Warren Buffet. The model that Buffet used was to actively manage one company and then using income from this active work to invest in opportunities for income that did not require *constant* active involvement. Using this model Buffet has been able to transform Berkshire Hathaway from a company that was about to go into bankruptcy when he purchased it into the 5th largest public company in the world – a company that for the past 49 years has seen the value of its shareholders investment to grow at an annual rate of nearly 20%![1]

The model that Buffet and Berkshire Hathaway used is one based upon the wise, studied, and thoughtful initial

---

[1] Warren Buffett. "Chairman's letter". Berkshire Hathaway 2012 Annual Report. p. 3. Retrieved March 13, 2013

investment of resources into business ventures that will provide future positive cash flow and return on investment with less future active involvement in the business venture. This future income stream will be from more passive involvement.

This same model is even more relevant, applicable, and useful today than it was five decades ago.

WHY MULTIPLE INCOME STREAMS

In our economic environment of today, it is very difficult for most working individuals to achieve financial independence using only the income and resources of our active, daily labors. Most of us are be required to use the income from our going to a work site and working in that job 40 or more hours per week in order to have the funds needed to buy food, clothing, and to have a house to live in.

The building of multiple income streams has become a necessity for most of us thought we might not recognize this. The continuing high rate of unemployment in most countries has taught us that no job is safe and secure. Unfortunately, most people only have the one source of income, that from their daily job – and that is proving to be a very risky situation. Even those couples in which both spouses work are often dependent upon the income from both. The sudden halt of one of those incomes will create major problems very quickly.

There is no limit as to the number of income streams you should have or create. The key is assure that the time and resources you spend maintaining an income stream does not become too unmanageable, continues to be worth the resources invested and spent, and that the income stream continues to produce a positive cash flow. There are several important advantages to creating numerous income streams, the first of which is to have some sort of income should your primary source of income suddenly cease. Even if your alternate sources of income do not cover all of your expenses, they may well lessen the impact of the unexpected job loss. Additionally, some income streams may have the potential to add to future savings rather than to only supplement current income.

WHAT IS PASSIVE INCOME

Fortunately, our business world and economic environment is also providing more and varied opportunities for individuals to create passive income streams. These passive income streams allow us to work our daily labors, which for most us are our primary sources of income, and to also be gaining additional income at the same time. In essence, these passive income streams are working for us while we are doing other work, activities, and sleeping. Passive income streams allow us to leverage our time and current active involvement with our previous resource investments and our wise decision-making. Notice the use of the word "leverage" in the previous sentence. There really is no 100% passive income stream. There will always be some maintenance to keeping an income stream working to its maximum level whether it is you that do the maintaining personally, or if you are trading for the required maintaining resources with someone else. Optimum performance of an income stream comes from how we leverage our time and our resources in "working" the income stream.

The simple idea of passive income is that it is income received with as little work as possible needed to maintain the stream of income once the initial work has been completed. Some traditional, commonplace examples of passive income are:

- Rent and lease from owned real estate properties
- Royalties on patents for an invention
- Fees received for trademark licensing for characters, creations, or brands that you created and registered
- Royalties from songs, books, publications, videos, other original works
- Dividends from stocks or other equity securities
- Interest from bonds, loans that you made, bank deposits, or other cash-like investments
- Retirement pensions

- Profits from ownership in businesses in which you have little or no active tasks or responsibilities
- Income from commissions on past sales of a product (i.e. insurance agent commissions, pyramid sales arrangements

However, with the advent and the evolution of the Internet communication systems, other forms of passive income are developing and becoming more accessible to more and more people. This 'online' focus of not only today's business world but also the changing character of how people across the globe are communicating, shopping, conducting business, learning, and exchanging information is providing more and more opportunities to earn income. Thus, new possible avenues of passive income are arising. These newer forms of passive income include:

- Earnings from Internet blogs, websites, or advertising
- eBook publishing
- eCourses
- Affiliated and Niche Websites
- Online Membership Sites and Programs
- Software Development (i.e. telephone and tablet apps, computer programs)
- Consultation Services
- Podcasts

However, as we will discuss, some of these advertised and promoted methods of passive income are not as passive or as lucrative as they are promoted to be.

WHY PASSIVE INCOME

Passive income is appealing because it allows you to spend your time doing things you enjoy as well as providing additional or needed income. Successful medical doctors, attorneys, or architects, for example, must continue to work the same number of hours at the same pay rate year after year if they desire to continue to maintain the same lifestyle. The same can be said for factory workers, retail salespeople, mechanics, and for most of us. And a worse scenario occurs when we can no longer work each day due to physical inability or the active work that we were doing is no longer needed or we desire to retire.

Traditionally, employees and self-employed business owners would contribute to company sponsored pension plans and to individual retirement and investment plans. But, the problem today is that most of these type plans are not growing or increasing in value enough to provide for a sustainable income should disability arise or retirement be desired. Compounding this lack of growth and increase in value of these traditional investments is that the cost of daily living has increased to such a level that the income from one individual's salary is not enough to take care of one's basic necessities and much less allowing for the investment of non-disposable monies into these slow growing investment accounts.

But with active development of passive incomes, significant passive income is possible. But as we will see, a significant investment of talent, time, money, or other resources is required.

Another characteristic of passive income that makes it appealing is the tax advantages that passive income often has over active income. Active income, in many national, state, and local jurisdictions is taxed at a higher rate than passive income. In the US, a business owner that works in his company has to pay large self-employment tax in addition to regular income taxes. Such a taxation system seems unfair, but this system provides incentive for individuals to invest in assets that create economic growth and that create jobs. A person that writes and publishes an eBook is providing a job for someone in the publishing company to "print", to "warehouse", to retail, and to distribute the book.

TWO GENERAL TYPES OF PASSIVE INCOME

There are two general types of passive income. Depending upon your financial situation, your talents, your skill set, your personality, and your life situation, the focus of which passive income type is best for you will change. The two general categories of passive income are:

- Those passive income sources that require considerable monetary capital to begin, maintain and grow
- Those passive income sources that do not require considerable monetary capital to begin, maintain, and grow

When focusing on the first type of passive income sources, we need money in hand or co-investors or the ability and willingness to take on large debts in order to finance the purchase of the initial investment assets. For instance, if purchasing rental property and we decide to take out a bank loan, we need to be certain that the generated cash flow from the rents of the property will cover all expenses of ownership as well as covering the loan payment. We also need to be as sure as possible that if we decide to dispose of the property in the future, that we will recoup our initial investment. Although the required personal equity in ventures such as this may only be a down payment of a few thousand dollars and those few thousand dollars will produce a large cash flow stream, there is some risk. If you cannot make the bank payments or cover the expenses of ownership, things can go badly very quickly.

Large investment portfolios are part of this first passive income type. Someone who owns $10 million dollars of stock in high-performing corporations, that person could reasonably expect to receive a half-million dollars a year in dividends. That person could lie on the beach every day and would still receive income from those companies as they paid their owners a portion of their earnings. But again we have the problem that it took $10 million dollars cash in hand to begin with.

Traditionally, the most customary path to generating large passive income streams has been to work at an active, primary job and to use part of that earned income to buy assets that will generate passive income. But as we have noted, unless there is considerable family resources or a very high income from the active job, it is becoming more and more difficult to buy such assets.

The second type of passive income sources – those passive income sources that require little monetary capital to begin, maintain, and grow – are probably better choices for those of us who desire to start out on our own and have very little capital to begin with. These passive income types allow us to create assets such as books, songs, videos, teaching curriculums, trademarks, Internet sites, recurring commissions, and to develop businesses that may continue to earn money after their initial creation. These businesses that eventually provide passive income are created by our investing of our current skills, talents, knowledge, and our time put into their creation.

PASSIVE INCOME MYTHS AND MISCONCEPTIONS

Like winning an Olympic medal or writing a best-selling novel, or earning a Pulitzer or Nobel Prize, receiving passive income requires work. At first glance, earning a Gold Medal or writing a book or earning an international prize may appear to be extremely different, yet each of them has a common requirement. This common requirement is also found with all types of passive income. That common requirement is knowledge.

Before we can ever begin to produce something of that will generate passive income we need to have not only specific knowledge of that something and but need to have some knowledge of what passive income is and we need knowledge of what passive income is not. To seek and to gain knowledge of all the advantages of passive income without investing equal time and energy to learning the disadvantages and requirements of earning passive income is fool-hearted and a sure route to disappointment. Let's take a look at few misconceptions of passive income:

- **Myth #1 – Get rich quick with little to no work or cash.** We all know, or should know, that there is no such thing as getting rich quickly, legally and legitimately, without a large investment of some sort of resource. (If there was, everyone would be doing it and it would soon cease to be that valuable and lucrative.) Passive income streams are based upon the resource investments of cash, skills and talents, and time. How much of one type of resource is dependent upon the investment of another resource type. If you have lots of money to invest, then you will probably need less time or skills to receive the same amount of passive income. If you have little cash, then you will need to invest more of your time or have a more valuable or marketable skill set or talent to use and invest with.

- **Myth #2 – You have to buy special tools.** To be a smart investor takes a reasonable amount of knowledge in the object in which you are investing. But there should be no reason for you to purchase books, DVDs, or pay for a seminar to learn how to invest. If the person or company that is offering you the opportunity to invest does not offer you all that you need to know to make a wise, knowledgeable and informed decision, that that person or company is probably not reputable and their offer is probably not legitimate. While many respected experts, professors, agents, and brokers do and have written books, those with integrity would not force someone to purchase such products in order to invest with them.

- **Myth #3 – An investment of your resources will guarantee a return.** Every investment has a certain amount of risk. We can minimize our risk by having as complete a knowledge as possible,

13

but even then there is always the unknown, unforeseen event can destroy the best of passive income sources. If you are not comfortable accepting the recognized risks and the possible loss of your cash and time resources after true, knowledgeable consideration, then do not invest in that passive income.

- **Myth #4 – Passive income does not require additional investments of resources after the initial investments.** Passive income does not mean that we can just sit around doing nothing and to forget about the passive income sources while the checks are automatically deposited into our bank accounts. Remember that this world is in constant flux. Every passive income source will need some maintaining. New ideas, new customer groups to target, changing the look of web sites, keeping the property maintained; there will always be the need for the investing of some combination of work, time, skills and talent, and cash to maintain the passive income. Either you will have to provide this maintenance investing or you will have to trade for it. If you do not do it yourself or trade for it, your passive income will dry up.

A REAL-WORLD, WORKING DEFINITION OF PASSIVE INCOME

With the dispelling of these myths and misconceptions, perhaps we can develop a real working definition of Passive Income:

> *Passive income is the money currently being generated from the past, initial investments of our cash, our skills and talents, and our time. This passive income may require a lesser continuing investment of resources than the original investment to maintain the same or increasing income return, but none-the-less, maintenance investment is required for passive income streams.*

THE REALITIES OF PASSIVE INCOME

There seems to be a swelling number of people, particularly younger people, who are in spellbound with the ostensibly limitless potential of the Internet and are now focusing their professional lives on acquiring passive income.

The fantasy they share goes something like this:

1) Write an eBook, or contract with a freelancer from a developing nation to research and write the book for you at an incredibly cheap rate on some niche subject.
2) Set up a Facebook and an AdWords campaign that targets the correct and best keywords as determined by the developing nation freelancers.
3) Use WordPress to put up a free landing page that is copy written by developing nation freelancers.
4) Initiate a pay-per-click campaign.
5) Wait for the money to flood in while napping on the beach.

With of all of the dog owners around the world buying your new eBook that tells how to keep their miniature dachshund from becoming overweight using Açai cleansings (the freelancer in the developing nation determined that pet health and antioxidant weight loss were hot search niches), you can simply email your freelance virtual assistant to make sure that transfers from your PayPal account are happening as you want them scheduled. And of course, all of this happens while you are not working but eating at the wonderful restaurant that your Internet research determined is trending this week on your particular Pacific island paradise.

Okay, perhaps the above is a little overboard with the caricatures. But really, it is not that much out of line with the popular definition of passive income that is being spouted in the circles of the young, techie groups who have placed passive income as their primary objective in their business and work lives.

However, there are a few problems you will face if passive income without active involvement has become your passion:

- **You cannot remain ahead of the competition passively.** If your meticulous research really does conclude that there is an amazing market niche that up to now has miraculously been unnoticed and unserved – such as dog owners who want to assist their canine pet to shed that extra weight naturally – eventually the word will get out that there is money to be made in this field and you will have competition. Someone will write a better eBook or develop a more attractive eCourse on pet training, or develop a better marketing campaign for antioxidant cleanses. You will probably find it to be very difficult to manage this competition without being active. And without managing the competition, you will find your market share going in the same direction as the Açai cleansing solutions.
- **You cannot retain a faithful population of customers passively.** As soon as your clients

realize that you are abandoning them they are going to think that you do not care for them, which may well be true. Those customers are going to start looking for another place or source for the product that you are providing.

- **You cannot develop and direct a great team of people passively.**

So, what is the biggest reality about passive income? Lasting passive income that makes us happy is not all that passive.

If you are planning to maintain a passive income that is profitable enough to keep you visiting your Pacific island paradise, you will need a growing, scalable business structure. You will need those freelancers mentioned above. But if you show no interest in being involved in the business, what kind of talent do you think you are going to attract and maintain? The people you will have working for you will be those people interested in only earning a quick dollar with as little involvement as possible. Perhaps they will be a mirror image of the person hiring them. But even if you attempt to hire someone to manage everything for you, a good talent is going to realize that you are adding zero value to the business and that good manager will begin to demand higher compensation or that good manager will realize that they can do all of this without you and will become your competition.

- **You cannot create meaning, or purpose or passion in your life passively.** As a business coach and consultant I have had opportunities to visit with many young entrepreneurs that have been able to earn income from being very passive in their passive income. They are traveling to the beach on a shoestring budget or sitting at home playing video games without being active in their business. However, the majority of these individuals are not happy. They tell me this. Though they do have some money flowing in from a passive income source, they are not very excited about. These people have made the mistake of equating earning money with the meaning for life. They have chosen to make money from something that brings no real enjoyment to them. They are making money from something that has no bearing or meaning to them. They have invested in a business that they want to distance themselves from as completely and as quickly as possible. They are hoping that the income from something that they care nothing about will buy them the opportunity to do something that they really care about. But they have things backwards.

I'm not attempting to be melodramatic. But the simple truth is money does not buy happiness. The best passive income sources are built upon those things that we like to do, that we want to be active in doing, and that we have a passion to be involved with.

What makes a business work is the creation of value. And the creation of value is an active process. Attempting to establish a business without you creating or contributing to the value of that business but thinking that this business will magically pay you money is just bad thinking. There are those people who have developed businesses that allow them to leverage their time in their creating value. These individuals have learned how to maximize their value of their time and have developed a working system to do that. However, they all began their businesses with personal investments of resources to develop those systems. They wanted to be actively involved in their businesses.

Think of the multi-millionaire and billionaire entrepreneurs. A great number of them do not every really leave their businesses though they certainly have enough real passive income to do so. They stay on because their businesses provide them with a meaning and a purpose for them doing what they are doing in their work.

Passive income is a bit like putting a rocket into space. It takes a lot of work, time, and energy in getting the rocket onto the launching pad. It takes more energy getting it into the air. And though once the rocket is in the upper atmosphere it takes less energy getting it moving, it continues to require energy in steering it.

And because it is fun to watch the rocket take off and to actually do what it has been programmed to do, I want to do it again.

CHAPTER TWO

DEVELOPING MULTIPLE INCOME STREAMS

If we have income flowing in each month form a freelance side business, from rental property, or from a specialty web site marketing a niche product, then we are no longer so dependent upon strictly the money from our daily job for our and our family's well-being. And if we have more than one additional income stream we are even that much less dependent. The idea is that the additional income streams should require less of our time and resources to maintain the cash flow from that income source.

Most people with full-time jobs work outside the home 35 to 40 hours per week. By managing their time well, most of working people can probably find another 15 so hours a week that they could be working without encroaching too much into family time. That is more than a week and a half of extra time each month that can be used to invest in an alternative income stream. What is needed to find this time is wise time-management and turning off the television.

Think of it this way, over the course of three months, those extra 15 hours per week aggregate into some 200 working hours. Or in another way of looking at it, we have the opportunity of working an additional four months every year. Now if we were to determine ourselves to diligently work for one month to establish an alternative income source, then we can establish four such income streams a year. Ideally, these income streams will also become more passive after they are established.

However, we need to be realistic. No income stream is ever completely passive. But if we choose the alternative income sources that we wish to develop wisely, then once that sources is established, we may be able to devote only a third as much time in their maintenance. After a year, we will then have three passive income streams that we are maintaining in our spare time.

What we need to do to make this multiple income stream goal succeed is to commit to establishing a new income stream every three months. The concept of multiple income streams works and has several benefits:

- It is less difficult to create several smaller income streams than one large one. there are more opportunities to passively earn $4000 a year than to passively earn $12,000 a year.
- Having multiple income streams with smaller incomes WILL REDUCE the impact of the loss of an income stream.
- In home businesses, you have more flexibility in your time with a wider division of income across multiple sources.

- We usually enjoy the work better as we are not bored by doing the same thing every day.
- Income streams are created with a greater focus and emphasis on our interests, talents and skills more than on amount of income.

While there are the advantages mentioned above to developing multiple income streams, there are some challenges:

- You need to practice good organization and time management. It can be difficult to keep note of the various tasks required to keep each income stream working without such organizational skills.
- You will need to find an effective balance so that enough attention is given to each income stream to maintain their growth and positive cash flow.
- Each start-up of the income stream business requires time and other resources.

In order to really capitalize on our time and resources, we need to shift our thinking a bit. Rather than considering that we are trading our current time for current money income, we will do better to view the time we expend on developing smaller, multiple income streams as opportunities to increase our per hour income in the near future and to have greater security in that income.

"Identifying an alternative income stream that will work for you"

FIRST QUESTIONS

Identified here are five questions that should be answered before you start the developing of any business income stream. These questions are personal and require honest reflection. Often times the success of failure of a business income stream is dependent upon the honest and thorough answering of these questions. Take some time with pencil and paper consider the following questions. These questions should stimulate ideas and creative thoughts that will help to guide you to the better business and income streams for your personality and situation. The questions are:

- What are my strengths, interests, and talents?
- Are there ways that I can use these strengths, interests, and talents to meet other people's needs now and in the future?
- What kind of business or what can I do that will allow me to use my strengths, interests, and talents that people will want to use in meeting their needs?
- Do I have any assets in hand that I can use in developing the business?
- Do I have the time to develop the business?

- Do I have the means to obtain any knowledge or assistance or resources that I may be lacking to establish the business?
- Will this business be one that will provide for more passive income once it is established?
- Is this a business that I can begin at home without having to take time and resources from my current job?

A good income stream for you should be recognizable because:

- you become enthusiastic and energetic when you think about doing the work,
- you can start doing right now or with some practice and or preparation, and
- there is a market for what you want to do.

NEXT STEPS

After deciding what type of business activity that you would like to become involved you will need to look at the resources that you have in hand right now. Do you have the resources or are the resources readily and inexpensively available that are needed to get the projected started? If you are looking at an Internet business, the answer is probably yes. However, for other projects, things maybe a bit more challenging.

What is next needed is the developing of a plan. Every successful business venture has a plan of some sort.

While luck and fortune has a place in all things, most luck and fortune is dependent upon how much thought and planning has gone into the venture. Using a standard business plan template is a good tool to start your planning.

A BUSINESS PLAN FOR A HOME BUSINESS ALTERNATIVE INCOME STREAM

1. **Project Description.** This initial section is where you decide exactly what this project is. You will describe what you are doing, why you are doing it, what differentiates this project from others, and what market need this project will be fulfilling.

2. **Market Analysis.** Before you actually start the developing of the project, it is imperative to do some research into your project's industry or discipline. You will want to look at what competitors are doing and how successful they are. You will want to determine if there is indeed a market that will provide the financial income you are seeking with this project.

3. **Organization & Management.** The organization may be extremely simple if you are the only person doing the work and making the decisions; however, you will still need to have some ideas of how to make decisions. You will need to have considered how money will flow, how bills will be paid, how many hours a week you will work on this project, when you will be doing the work, etc.

4. **Service or Product Line.** What exactly are you going to sell? What is the lifecycle of the product? Will you be able to modify or add on to the product?
5. **Marketing & Sales.** How do you plan to market the product or service? Describe your sales strategy. Investigate marketing outlets.
6. **Resources.** What resources will you need and at what time in the development process will you need those resources? Are the resources available? If not, how and when do you anticipate acquiring the needed resources?
7. **Financial Projections.** What are reasonable expectations of income from this project? How long will this project be cash positive? Will the return be worth the investment? Be sure to include your time worth when considering your return on investment.

As you complete you project plan you will find yourself in two roles. You will be the energetic let's-get-this-going person and you will also be the let's-stop-and-think-about-this person. Both personal roles are needed to formulate a good and well-thought out plan. It is while you are doing this plan that the final decision of moving forward with your project or not should be made. As you were making your decision about what type of project to develop you found yourself looking at your capital resources. As already discussed, the amount of capital resources available to us has a major impact on what type of income stream project we will invest in.

28

CHAPTER THREE:

INVESTMENT STREAMS REQUIRING LITTLE CAPITAL INVESTMENT

Many of us simply do not have a great deal of cash to invest in an alternative income stream. As attractive and as profitable real estate and rental income is, getting started in that business requires considerable cash. You have to have cash for that initial down payment, closing costs, and initial couple of months operating expenses. However, there are some income stream projects that require little initial capital investment. Many of these income streams also have the potential to provide more passive income. And many of these low capital investment income streams with passive income potential are Internet based. This Internet is increasingly making these income stream projects possible, available, and suitable to a wide range of different business industries, disciplines, and applications. Many people from many walks of life, experiences, education backgrounds, and skill sets are able to identify and develop income streams using the Internet and computer technology as the basis for marketing, production, and distribution of a product or service.

Let's take a look at a few of these possible income stream projects.

FREELANCING

Freelancing is the practice of doing a job or a task for a paying party but without having a long-term commitment to that paying party. Freelancers are usually contracted to complete a particular project or assignment and receive compensation for the successful completion of the assignment or project. Freelancers, as self-employed, independent contractors, usually have greater flexibility in how to complete a project than a salaried employer.

Freelancers are may also be represented by a company or agency that markets and sells the freelancers labor. This companies or agents may or may not offer project management assistance or other contributions and assistance to the freelancer with the contracted assignment or project. An example of this type of arrangement could be a fashion model or an actor.

Some common fields and discipline that in which for freelancing include:

Copywriting, Publishing, Acting, Photography, Photojournalism, Film making, Music, Cosmetics, Editing, Proofreading, Copy editing, Computer programming, Video editing, Journalism, Website design and development, Business consulting, Book writing, Screenwriting, Event management and planning, Cosmetics and fragrances, Graphic design, Language translating, Transcription, Illustrating and Tour guiding.

FREELANCE METHODS AND COMPENSATION

The most common freelance field of work involves writing of some sort with nearly fifty percent of all freelancers showing this as their primary skill. The next three top freelancing fields are translating, web development, and marketing.[2]

How the freelancer works with his or her client depends upon the industry. Freelancing business consultants will often have written contracts with their clients; these contracts outlining compensation and depending upon performance. Freelance journalists, writers, and photographers will often work with an agreement for pay after the successful completion and acceptance of the project or task. Freelancers will often do speculative or free work for a publisher in order to establish credibility, a reputation, and a marketable portfolio. For large or time-consuming projects, it is common for freelancers to provide estimates of time and cost before beginning a project. Milestones, or points in the progression of the project, are commonly established and deposits or partial payment for the project is made when those milestones are reached.

The method of compensation for the freelancer is also field and industry dependent. Compensation could be set by time on the job, which is common for filmmaking crews and concert production technicians. Payment

---

[2] Gandia, E. (2012). Freelance Industry Report. International Freelancers Academy.

could also be for each piece produced or by the project which is common for freelance writers. A current trend among freelance Internet marketers is value-based pricing in which the marketer does a project without promise of any payment, doing "spec" work, and then showing the results of the marketer's labors to the seller of the product being marketed and asking for compensation based upon the client's perception of those results. However, in any of the compensation schemes that freelancers use, there is not guaranteed payment for their work.

In artistic fields such as writing and video and film making, freelancers may retain the copyright of their works while selling the right to publish the works under a time-limited contract. Or the freelancer may work as an independent contractor that has been hired to create a certain work. These freelancers may contractually give all the intellectual rights to the produced work to the entity paying the contract. This latter arrangement is common for ghostwriters and copywriters.

BENEFITS TO FREELANCING

There is no one reason that freelancers list for working as freelancers. The perceived benefits for freelancing are wide and varied and with the differences based upon the lifestyle, the gender, and the industry of the individual freelancer. Two of the often cited benefits are time and scheduling flexibility and the ability to work in a field that the freelancer feels passionate about. There are also some industries and disciplines that rely primarily upon freelance labor rather than full-time employees (i.e. journalism, modeling). Freelancing has recently grown due to workers that have lost their regular jobs in the current economy changes. Many of these workers have been talented and skilled in areas such as accounting, finance and marketing.

DRAWBACKS TO FREELANCING

Just like temporary and part-time work, freelancing can be precarious. Finding steady, continuous, and good-paying work is not assured. Until a freelancer has developed a reliable and large enough clientele, the freelancer will likely have some unproductive time. There is also the continual problem with clients that do not pay on time. In the writing and artistic industries, especially those freelancers that sign non-disclosure agreements and assign all the copyrights of a work to paying party, there has been an increase in the paying party accepting copies of the works for "review", declaring the work unacceptable and then not rendering payment. However, that same unaccepted work is still published by the original contractor and the freelancer has no legal recourse due to the signed contract. Another drawback to freelancing is the lack of benefits, especially health insurance if the freelancer lives in a country such as the US where universal health care does not exist.

Freelancers that live in countries with developed economies usually do not earn as much as their employed resident counterparts. Most freelancers have attained several years of experience in their field before going independent. However, even the very experienced freelancers do not always earn an income equal to that of a full-time employee. Freelancers report that many prospective clients offer very low rates while demanding very high standards for the work. Because of the competitive bidding for most projects, many knowledgeable professional freelancers simply do not bid due to the extreme undercutting of unprofessional freelancers.

IS BEING A FREELANCER A DOABLE CAREER FOR YOU?

There is the concept of an alternative income stream, there is the enjoyment of varied work and work that you really like, and there is the possibility of having more control over your working day. So, who would not want to be a freelancer? These are attractive sounding advantages; however they are only from one side of freelancing. If we set aside the unfortunate fact that economic necessity obliges some people into freelancing, freelancing is not a career choice or even an alternative income stream for everyone.

SOME BASIC POINTS TO CONSIDER FIRST

It does not matter if you are thinking of embarking upon a new career as a freelancer or if you are looking to just do some freelancing as a side job to supplement your income, there are a few items to think about before you start working on that catchy logo for your web page. And do not allow the all the advantages blind you to the disadvantages.

As we have already mentioned to some degree, there are some big differences between freelancing and having a salaried job. The knowledge that there is no promise of a paycheck being deposited into your checking account each week should be the first thing to catch your attention. There is also the knowledge that you have to seek out and locate your own work. And in the process of finding and securing that work, you have to figure out how much to charge for that work so that you do not go into the red. Then there are the deadlines that you must meet if you want to work again for that client. And when that client is completed, you have to find another and start the process all over again.

Then there is also the balancing act that freelancers must master. A freelancer is in all practicality a corporation with one employee. The freelancer is

- the marketing department that is advertising your skill set, abilities, and availability

- the sales department that closes the deal with the potential client
- the accounting department that takes care of the invoicing, the checking on payments, the moving of funds in the bank accounts, the paying of bills, the tax reporting, and the assuring that a profit is being made
- the customer service department that makes sure client relationships are smooth and pleasant
- the IT department that has to deal with software glitches and modem and router problems
- and then, finally, you get to be the operations department that actually does the work

The freelancer is also responsible for training and learning and keeping up with all that is necessary to not only do the contracted tasks but to also stay ahead of your competition. If you are behind or if you fall behind in your skill set, you will fail. Any mistakes made in the operation of the business are your fault. To be a freelancer requires more than just being an expert in your field or area. You have to be a generalist in running a business. Freelancers are usually very well-rounded in their knowledge, experiences, and skills. Ask yourself the question, are you well rounded in your business aptitudes and experience as well as an expert in your field?

Finding work to do

Companies, corporations, and small businesses are discovering that restructuring into leaner organizations with less redundancies and less overhead is a requirement for today's economy. This restructuring is producing more freelance work out there. But this same restructuring is also putting more people into the world of freelancing. Simply finding a job could be a difficult job. Consider carefully your possible clients. Will there be enough clients and will there be enough potential work to keep you working? Will the work pay enough to be worth your efforts? What strategy will you use to position yourself ahead of the competition? Are you able to market yourself? In addition to your existing clients, you will need to constantly be marketing yourself to new clients.

Your skill set

Assess your skills and experience and abilities. Do you have something that others require or desire? The higher demand for the work that you can do, the more opportunities to work you will have and the higher compensation for your work you can ask for. This is one of the reasons that freelancers often do not embark as freelancers until later in their careers. Clients seek freelancers to do the jobs and tasks that they cannot. Consequently, it is those freelancers that have extensive CVs with a variety of knowledge, skills, and abilities (KSAs) that clients go to most often.

Expected compensation

You need to closely examine how much you must earn monthly and then truly gauge if you will be able to earn that as a freelancer. The estimated rates for work may sound very inviting, but there will be days in which you do not have work. You must enter holidays, sick time, and other not working time when estimating your potential income.

Paying yourself less than you earn

There is usually a difference between the salary that we must earn and the salary that we want to earn. As salaried workers that earn a set salary each month, we have the tendency to spend all of a paycheck by the time the next paycheck arises. We set our budgets in that way because we know that will be getting another paycheck. But as a freelancer, because you are not guaranteed a regular paycheck, you should only pay yourself the absolute minimum that you need to live on. When, or if, you grow a big enough emergency fund to allow some splurges even after covering a lot of non-working days, then you splurge.

There is no regular payday

For many of us waiting a month on the next paycheck is difficult. However, freelancers may go two to three months between pay checks. And during this time the household bills are still coming in. A month can seem a long time as you try and manage a monthly budget out your monthly salary, but imagine waiting several months for payment while your own bills are mounting up. If you are writing a book or magazine articles, some publishers do not complete pay until after the magazine or book has hit the street. For this reason, having at least three and preferably six months' salary in the bank is a good idea for freelancers.

Keeping deadlines

Yes, freelancing does offer an opportunity to liberate you from the stressful nine to five work week. However, you still have to do the work at some time between midnight and midnight. Your clients will still need and demand that you provide the work they need done when you agreed to provide it to them. If you want to spend the daylight hours fishing or sitting on the beach, do it. But be prepared to not to sleep that night because you will need to be working. It is that simple. If you do not meet the deadlines, you will have a lot of time to sit on the beach. The problem will be paying for the piña colada.

Freelancing is not a job where you get paid for doing nothing. The more you work, the more you get paid. The more projects that you complete, the more time you have to work; more work means more money. If you are the type person that consistently uses all of the available time to finish a project, then you will have more difficulty surviving as a freelancer.

Managing your time

Freelancers are realistic about the amount of work that can do. Having a good idea of how long it will take you to complete a project is a must for bidding on projects and having those projects that are worth the effort and time. Freelancers also know that it is sometimes best not to take on a very lucrative project if they are already heavily time involved with a current project. To renege on a project is freelance suicide. Freelancers know how not to overburden themselves.

Marketing yourself

Your clients will not only appraise you on the quality of your earlier work but also on the recommendations and review of previous clients. How will you present yourself to potential clients? Will your previous clients recommend you to others? Do you have a portfolio and reference list? Do you have a website? Are you using social media to advertise yourself?

Are you determined and disciplined?

There will be times in which situations and circumstances cause a deadline to be very close and you will still have lots of work to do on the project. Working around the clock and ignoring the things you want to do to meet the pressing deadline are sometimes required of a freelancer. Can you just say no to the televised ballgame or going out with the family if there is work to be done? Can you go on four hours sleep for a couple of days? The very nature of freelancing means working when you can and sleeping when there is no work. Flexibility is a benefit of the job, but it is also a necessary, disciplined trait for freelancers.

Can you work alone?

Freelancers usually do not work in offices that are a bevy of social activity. The freelancer is usually working alone. Freelancers have to do without knowing the latest gossip or group discussions about last evening ball game. Working alone does not suit everyone.

MARKETING YOURSELF AS A FREELANCER

As an employee that is not directly involved with marketing and advertising, you probably did not give that much attention or even think much about marketing. The work was just there for you each day to complete. You did your part in the production of a product or service that was sold and you received your pay for it. However, there was someone in the organization that was thinking of marketing. The organization had some method of letting people know that they had a product available. In some organizations, there is a marketing department, in others the marketing is handled by outside companies. But in both cases, there was someone in the organization making sure that marketing was happening and that made sure the marketing was successful.

What is marketing?

Marketing is the management process that takes a product or service from the initial conceptual idea of the product or service to the placing it in front of the customer in such a manner that the customer will desire and be able to purchase the product. This management process of often illustrated in four particular elements that are referred to as the four P's of marketing:

1) **product** identification, selection and development,
2) **pricing** of the product,
3) **placing** the product in front of the customer through advertising channels, and
4) **promoting** the product through directed strategies

An example of this marketing management is Apple. Apple's products are conceived and developed to include not only improved applications but also new applications to meet newly perceived needs of the targeted market groups. The varying prices for the different products are established depending upon the capabilities that the customer desires in each product. New Apple products are sold in places where current and older Apple products are sold. Apple promotes its products as major technical breakthroughs at special debut shows and in tech magazines and journals. Other promotion includes high volume advertising in social and other web media and in print and television outlets.

Marketing is the consideration of the customer's needs and the customer's satisfactions with the product. This consideration is different than the idea of selling a product.

> *"Selling concerns itself with the tricks and techniques of getting people to exchange their cash for your product. It is not concerned with the values that the exchange is all about. And it does not, as marketing invariable does, view the entire business process as consisting of a tightly integrated effort to discover, create, arouse and satisfy customer needs."*[3]

As Professor Levitt is telling us, marketing is less concerned with getting customers to pay for a product and more concerned with developing a product that meets a customer's needs and in creating a demand for that product.

So how does marketing relate and translate into a part of freelancing?

For freelancers, the four P's can be view like this:

- **Product** is what you are offering to your client
- **Price** is the compensation that you desire for the product you are offering your client

---

[3] Levitt, Theodore. *The Marketing Imagination*. New York: Free Press, 1983. Print.

- **Place** is the actual location or method of presenting the product offer to the customer
- **Promotion** is the discussion with and the convincing of the customer that your product is of value and worth the price and that the customer should purchase your product

Also, these four Ps are rudimentary and may not be sufficiently expanded to include all of the elements necessary to marketing your product. There are also the **people** that you will be targeting with your product. You may want to consider the **proven** or **physical** evidence of your product's quality when promoting the product. The important idea for the freelancer is to use the interplay of these marketing elements to let people know that you have a product that they can use. Marketing is not simply having a web site or a YouTube video. Those are the outcomes and tools of marketing. Marketing is a process; a process that you need to entrench in your freelancing adventure from the very outset. Creating detailed marketing plans as part of your original business plan is a key asset in effective marketing.

Product pricing

To get pricing right you must do some research. As part of your business plan you should have determined how much of a demand is there for your product among your targeted customer group. You should have also looked at competition. What is the quality of your competition's products relative to your product? Are does the competition market themselves? Are they marketing themselves as discount and value vendors or are they promoting themselves as the premium and superior purveyors for their products? How will you be promoting yourself relative to the competition? You should take a good look at the competition's prices. After considering your cost for producing the product, can you price compete with the competition? Will selling your product at the expected or determined price be worth your efforts?

This same approach can be used when you expand with other products or move into other markets. As you develop your freelance business you will probably notice the need for niche products that you can develop and provide.

And when you are determining your product price do not forget to consider any commissions paid to agencies or distribution costs.

The rates you charge need to reflect what it costs you to be in business and to produce the product. Be careful not to underestimate all associated costs including start-up costs, ongoing expenses, and future investments in capital assets and equipment.

Freelancers will also find that there are times in which pricing a product a bit low in order to get their product in front of a potential high-volume client. Freelance writers will often take on a single project with a publisher at a discounted rate with the knowledge that this publisher will have several more projects coming in the near future. Once the freelance writer's work is seen to be of very high quality, the publisher is often more apt to extend an invitation to the freelancer and the freelancer may be able to ask for a higher rate.

Position

Positioning yourself refers to the creation of an identity for your business. Successful freelancers stand out from other freelancers. They are distinctive. They are easily recognizable. Many freelancers simply use their own name and do not develop a "brand name". Their own name becomes their brand. But even in using your own name, you will need to help clients understand what your products are and then to promote yourself in accordance to those products. If you are a CPA that specializes in working with high-wealth individuals that live in New York, then you will need to position yourself as such. You will want your name mentioned at the polo club and at the parties in Southampton more so than among the vendors on Coney Island. When your name is mentioned at the polo club, you want people to know who you are.

If you have created a limited corporation or company or if you have multiple products or services or if want greater awareness of your freelance company, then you may want to go with a branded company name. But again, a brand name is much more than a catchy name and a logo. A brand is the psychological and emotional relationship that you have with your customers. I own and drive Toyotas. The brand has proven itself over and over to me for thirty years that its products meet my needs and expectations. The Toyota brand conveys certain traits about its business and products. The same should be said for a freelancer when positioning him or herself in their chosen market.

What's in a Brand name?

If you are creating a brand name, keep the name truthful and simple. Don't call yourself *Total Computer Solutions* if you only work on Mac's. Consider what your values are and what you do. Try to find a name that reflects those values and your products. If you are a traditional, academic writer do not attempt to present yourself as a tongue-in-cheek satirist. Some personality should be expressed in your brand name. Original and succinct names are ideal. Do not use unstylish, outmoded, or clichéd names. Would you really want to use a CPA that works for *Tax breakers* or hire a writer from *Words R Us*? And attempt to make sure that the name you choose is not already being used.

Creating your brand identity

You may find it beneficial to have a designed logo for your business cards, letterheads, and shipping materials. To save some cash early on, you might want to design the logo yourself using available software and available talent. However, after the business has grown a bit and is starting to expand by word of mouth and referrals, then you may want to invest a few dollars into a professionally produced logo and logoed materials. This might be a great task for a fellow freelancer.

Promotion

The promotion element of marketing is like the upper part of an iceberg, it only compromises about ten percent of the marketing efforts but it is the visible ten percent. The initial and the primary step in the freelancer's promotion efforts should be determining what the target customer group is. By efficiently and decidedly making this initial determination, you will be able to save considerable time and resources by not promoting your product to people who will simply do not have a need for it or will not ever buy it. Most people will never be in a position to need or have a desire to buy a Rolls Royce or a Learjet. Due to the nature of their products, neither BMW nor Bombardier, the current makers of the cars and the planes, do not promote their products to the majority of the public; rather they specifically target the ultra-rich and the major corporations. That does not mean that only their targeted customer groups know of their companies and products. It simply means that they are attempting to make their products desirable and buyable for those groups. Though I am not on the Rolls' mailing list, if I ever have a need for a $300,000 car, I know that they have a product that might work for me.

Before beginning the promotion phase of marketing and as you continually do your promoting, attempt to answer the following questions:

- Who will or who is likely to buy your product?
- What are some common characteristics that your best customers share with each other?
- Are you able to reach all of your clients using the same communication outlets and channels?
- Do your clients fall into different groups?
  - If yes, what differentiates the groups? Do they have different buying habits?

Once you know who your customers are then you will be able to determine effective channels for communicating your message to them.

ADVICE FOR BECOMING A DEPENDABLE AND SUCCESSFUL FREELANCER

We already mentioned the growing competition in the freelance world. And the adage 'you are only as good as your last job' resounds very true in the freelance marketplace. The most desirable trait that good clients want in a freelancer is dependability. That is the key to becoming a successful freelancer. Dependability will beat out random brilliance every time. The freelancer is an intermittent resource that does not have to be used. To be used consistently, the freelancer has to provide the advertised quality of work each time the client calls. So what are some things that successful freelancers do that make them successful?

1) **Produce and deliver good work.** A successful freelancer will have a high quality of work every time. There are occasions in which the freelancer might be less than equal to past performance, but these should be rare exceptions. Common reasons for a dip in quality are accepting too much work, a misunderstanding of the project brief, or not having adequate knowledge or experience in the project area. Successful freelancers take great care in avoiding these common problem areas. Successful freelancers resist the temptation to turn out substandard work. Substandard work will have your name removed from a client's freelancer roster. And in many cases, you will have to redo the substandard work that you were originally hired to complete.

2) **Produce and deliver work according to the project brief.** A project brief should be a clear and defined description of the work that is to

be completed. Ask questions when the brief is not clear and defined. Ask for clarification of anything that you are unsure of. Ask your questions via email. All replies should also be in writing. This procedure assures that everyone knows exactly what is expected and prevents future misunderstandings. This also allows for the freelancer to verify that the work being done is what is expected without continually asking the client the same question numerous times. As the project progresses and if things that need to be amended or unasked questions arise, be proactive and contact the client as needed.

3) **Maintain contact with the client and keep the client informed of project developments.** Successful freelancers keep the client informed of how things are going. No client likes un-enjoyable surprises. Likewise, most clients like some assurance that the project is going well. The 'no news is good news' maxim is not one for freelancers to practice. The longer the project, the more important it is to provide updates and progress reports. Use these reports to submit working drafts of projects to assure that the work is aligned to the project brief. There may be some projects in which there is nothing to report during a time period. However, an email will keep the client assured that you are doing your job thus letting the

client to have one less concern. This is especially true if your project is part of a larger project that the client is managing. If there are problems on your end, the client may need to make adjustments in other areas of the project. Waiting to the last minute to break bad news to a client will assuredly cause the loss of a client.

4) **When you have to present problems from your end, present them with possible solutions.** Problems do occasionally come up. Clients accept that fact. However, as the person most knowledgeable in the project work and with the greatest knowledge of the problem, the freelancer is probably in the best position to offer a workable solution. And even if the solution is not workable, the freelancer is being proactive, showing a great concern for the project, and is willing and wanting to make the problem right.

5) **Be a proactive and self-sufficient.** The nature of freelancing is that you are assigned tasks that a client does not have the resources to complete. The client may lack the staffing, the time, or the know-how to do the task. You advertised yourself as having those things. Hence, the client expects you to be able to complete the task with a minimum of questions. The project brief is when you should ask the great majority of your questions. This does not mean that you should not ask needed

questions when they arise, but a successful freelancer will anticipate obvious questions and situations and ask them during the brief.

6) **Turn around work quickly.** There are occasions in which clients need something done quickly and done well. When those occasions come up, clients will go to those freelancers that have been quick and good in the past. Turning in a quality project within a tight deadline puts your name at the top of the client's freelance roster. And next time that kind of job comes up, you will be in position to ask a premium rate.

7) **Be flexible and adaptable.** Though commonly solitary workers, successful freelancers have the capability to move seemingly effortlessly into a team position. This flexibility is demonstrated in those long-distance client relationships where only emails and phone calls are traded and also in those projects in which the freelancer works inside the client's workplace. Each client and client team is different with its own personality and quirks and practices. The ability to adapt to each team and workplace allows the freelancer to start work immediately without creating conflict among the client's staff and keeps the freelancer from feeling aloof and clumsy. Being flexible and adaptable in the current project goes far in getting you the next project with that client. Successful freelancers are not flies

on the wall. Rather successful freelancers ask what they can do to help, they look for opportunities to contribute to the next project or the next stage in the project and they let people know that they are available for those opportunities.

8) **Deliver value for the client's money.** This concept does not mean that you will always have to be the cheapest freelancer in town. When you provide a good service for a just compensation, you are adding value to the project and to the client's investment. If you have better skills, more experience, and greater talent than the competition and can show that, then do so. This is showing the client that the value you offer is higher than the cheaper competitor.

9) **Continually increase the value of the products you offer.** This is done by adding to your knowledge, skills, and abilities. As every business is in constant change, the successful freelancer keeps up with changes in the field and area as well as staying aware of changes in the organizations of regular clients. Adding new skill sets takes time. Setting aside time for career development is paramount. And new skill sets will allow for a broader range of projects for you to undertake as well as adding quality to the current project and work areas; thus increasing income potential. However, be

prudent in what skill sets you are adding. There is no reason or benefit to learn something that is redundant, of no use or value, or will quickly be obsolete.

10) **Monitor customer satisfaction and make changes based upon feedback.** Having a quick conversation at the end of a project will tell you a lot about the client's feelings on a project. You can take a more formal customer satisfaction survey by adding one with your invoice. By assuring that the client is completely satisfied with the project you are not only learning what you can do better but you are also reminding the client of what a good job you did and you are placing yourself in a great position to be chosen for that client's next job.

11) **Service after the project.** Provide professional invoices and reports promptly. If a client has legitimate follow-up questions about resources, processes used, and other matters pertaining directly to the work, answer them promptly, without giving up your trade secrets.

12) **Maintain an open dialogue with clients.** Keep clients advised about what you are doing. Email them when you have added new projects or upgraded your skills. If you have recently completed a big project, let them know of your accomplishment. This will keep you in the front

of their mind even in those times in which you do not have a current project with them.

Freelancers provide an invaluable service and contribution to so many different areas of business and creativity. Those freelancers that are sincerely dedicated to serving clients and making worthwhile contributions are not only welcome in the industry but are needed to keep freelancing as a professional occupation. And freelancing can be a great alternative income stream.

SELF-PUBLISHING

With the Internet and its access to communication channels, many authors are choosing to self-publish. They are bypassing established third-party publishers with themselves taking on the tasks of getting the book to print and marketing the book. The author takes on all the responsibilities and assumes control of designing, printing, pricing, distributing, marketing, and promoting the work. The author has the option of doing all the work or outsourcing some of those services. Self-publishing commonly includes paper books, eBooks, websites, pamphlets, and teaching materials.

But before you get too excited about the possibility of having an income stream via authoring and self-publishing a book, here is some advice from a current *New York Times* best-selling author and self-publisher that has earned a great deal of money. Guy Kawasaki offers this:

Write a book because you have something important to say. If you have a life story that inspires, or information that you believe everyone in a particular niche NEEDS to know, then do it... ...someone should not rush to get something out because it might enhance a career, profile, business, or bank account. You just won't succeed with those inner motives. If you're thinking just about what you can get out of it, you're probably writing a 'crappy' book.[4]

On that note, the advice of some small business and entrepreneurial coaches to throw together any book as quickly as possible and to get it into print to make money flies in the face of good, wise advice. Think about it. Unskilled carpenters and other such trade crafters who produce shoddy products rarely make any money and will be derided by their customers for years to come. Writers can fall into the same category.

THE BUSINESS OF SELF-PUBLISHING

The strategic distinguishing trait of self-publishing is choosing to publish a work independently of traditional publishers. Historically, independent publishers invested sizeable quantities of money in preparing a

---

[4] Caprino, Kathy. "Considering Self-Publishing? Don't Bother, Unless You Follow Guy Kawasaki's Advice." Forbes. January 21, 2013. Accessed September 14, 2014.

manuscript for print, printing bulk quantities of the book or work, and in storage and distribution of the printed copies. Print-On-Demand (POD) and electronic book (eBook) technologies now allow the author or independent publisher to have a book or work printed or digitally produced, distributed and sold only after an order has been placed; thus, lowering expenses and capital asset investments significantly.

Print-On-Demand publishing is the publisher's capability to physically print high-quality paper books only as needed. Rather than running hundreds of books and having to deal with delivery and warehousing of the books and pay those costs, POD allows for a book to be made available and to pay for the expense of its printing and distribution only after it has been ordered.

EBook publishing is the publication of a book-length work in a digital format. This format allows the book, including text and images, to be read on computers and other electronic devices. Originally designed to be an electronic version of an already printed book, many eBooks are now published without a printed version of the book. EBook formats include the ability to be read on nearly any sophisticated device such as a smartphone, computer, or tablet computer or they can be published in a format that is viewable only on a dedicated device. Amazon's Kindle is an example of this formatting.

Self-publishing has never been easier or quicker. Traditional publishers prior to the past few years would commonly take a year or longer to turn a manuscript into a printed book, and that was after it was accepted. And having your book accepted was not an easy thing. In fact, getting just a synopsis of your work in front of a publisher to review was very difficult. However, with the Internet and eBook publishing and publishers, it is possible to have your manuscript available for sale to customers just about anywhere in the world in less than an hour. But the real battle is still the same now as it has already been for writer. That battle and problem is finding a reading audience.

There will continue to be a need for using traditional publishing houses for many authors. There are some types of books, such as academic writings, textbooks, and specialty writings, which require considerable amount of research time, research expenses, and have a very limited reading audience. These works will need the support for marketing, publicizing, and distributing these works that only the large publishers can offer. But there is a wider reading audience that favors fiction works, food and drink books, and do-it-yourself (DIY) books, all genre which easily fit into self-publishing.[5] Granted, the number of books that are being sold and read in the US is dropping. However, international book sales are increasing.[6] So while there is debate about the

---

[5] Rogers, S., & Rowling, J. (2012, December 28). *Top 100 bestselling books of 2012*. Retrieved September 13, 2014.

viability of eBook publishing continuing to be a lucrative income stream for US and English only books, there is a growing international market and for books in languages other than English.

Writing and self-publishing a book as an income stream is a wonderful opportunity for many people, but it is not for everyone for various reasons. Despite the popular belief and truism that everyone has a story to share, not every story is highly interesting to a lot of people. Many people simply do not have the gift of writing. Those that do not will have to find someone to write their story for them and then we get into balancing the costs of hiring ghostwriters versus sales and things like that. However, for those who do have a good story, particular expertise and knowledge that is marketable, or that can absorb knowledge from many different sources and then to package this knowledge into a more concise, usable and readable bundle, then self-publishing is something to consider.

However, eBook publishing is not an immediate and huge windfall for most independent publishers. The income from a single publication is usually quite small – yes, I know this is something that is not spoken of in most self-publishing books and articles – but it remains to be true. Most books will reach the 90% mark of

---

[6] "Book Sales Statistics." - Amazon, Barnes&Noble and Book Store Sales Numbers Annual Update. February 1, 2014. Accessed September 13, 2014.

lifetime sales within five years. Most eBooks being self-published are generating less than $3000 a year for the publisher. Hence, a single published eBook is not going to earn a lot of money. However, if you publish four such books a year, then you are starting to get into some better money. And as more passive income, the published book holds an edge over freelancing and other income sources. If you were to publish only four books a year and only made a profit of $1000 per book per year, after five years you would have a more passive income stream of $16,000 per year. If you consider that you are doing this because you like to write and to publish and are doing it in your spare time, then that is a decent extra income for many of us.

Most people will not become rich solely through self-publishing a half-dozen eBooks. However, most people who have the ability to write and to self-publish a few books can develop a supplemental income stream that can become more passive.

And the best part about self-publishing for the aspiring author is all of those things that are not dependent upon selling the book: doing something you like, writing your story, learning new things, the satisfaction of accomplishment, and the adding of value to your life and to the lives of others.

SELF-PUBLISHING A BOOK

As mentioned, there can be great opportunity in being your own publisher; especially if you have one of the mentioned gifts: a marketable story, a talent for writing, or the ability to "re-communicate". But the writing is certainly not the only part of self-publishing. That is only the beginning. Nearly all successful authors are required to do non-writing tasks in order to sell their books. And if you are also your own publisher, the list of non-writing tasks is increased even more.

PLANNING YOUR BOOK - SELECT THE CORRECT BOOK, A FITTING GENRE AND THE APPROPRIATE TITLE

Good writers who write good works write for the right reason. They write because writing is part of them. If writing is a chore, then writing is probably not something that you will be successful at.

That being said, let's continue on.

The first step is to decide what kind of book you will be writing. Is it fiction or non-fiction? If fiction, will the work be a novel or something shorter? You must consider your audience no matter what type of book you decide to write. Who is the target audience and what do you wish the target audience to get from the reading of your book? Are you attempting to entertain only? What kind of entertainment? Do you wish to teach a skill or to help the reader overcome a problem? Do you wish to impart knowledge to the reader?

If you have chosen to write a book that is more in the line of an elegant work of literary fiction, or if the subject is more esoteric (i.e. hummingbirds, nanotechnology), or if the book will be a children's book, then you will probably be better in staying with a more traditional publisher that has experience in those books. In today's digital and electronic literary markets, most successful eBooks come from the popular and pop-culture genres. These genres already have major online communities that are easier to market into. These genres include horror/crime/techno thrillers, fantasy/science/future fiction and romance/erotica/women's fiction. Self-help and DIY are good non-fiction genres.

A working title should be distinctive but not baffling.

THE WRITING

Let us start this section with this statement: It has to be good!

This rule applies to print books or self-published books. If you do not have a good book to begin with, you will have very little hope in selling it.

SO, WHAT MAKES A BOOK GOOD?

That is a very subjective question. To delve deeply into that discussion is outside the purview of this book. However, in order to give the reader of this book some assistance in deciding if writing or publishing a specific book is a promising project to undertake, here are some general concepts.

In the realm of fiction, there are four general elements that readers look for regardless of the genre or book style:

- **An interesting voice.** A writer's voice is the individualized style of writing that an author uses in a work. It is combination of diction, syntax, punctuation, dialogue, character development, and other literary devices. For most readers, voice is the most important element of a good book because the voice permeates through every sentence of the book. If the writer does not connect with the reader through the book's voice, it really does not matter how good the storyline is, the reader will not buy the book.
- **Memorable characters.** In most fiction genres, it is the characters that make the story memorable. The characters are what the reader connects with in the book's story. Believable characters are what people identify with.
- **A vivid setting.** The book's settings should feel real. Even in a fantasy world, a good writer will make the setting seem believable. Vivid settings

revealed through vivid descriptions are a memorable as the events that happen there.

- **A gripping story.** Regardless of the characters, or the setting, it is what is happening that keeps a reader awake until two in the morning reading a book. The plot and storyline are where word-of-mouth recommendations come from. Great characters in vivid locations that are doing nothing interesting will not sell a book.

In the realm of non-fiction, a good book will have these elements:

- A timely or timeless subject that is imparted in a distinctive manner that is thought-provoking and appealing to a broad audience.
- A title that is descriptive, illustrative, attracts attention, and invites queries.
- A well-written body that has been edited with strict attention to sentence structure, grammar, and spelling. The terminology and vocabulary is made understandable to the layperson with an avoidance of slang and out-of-place idioms.
- The author is an expert or professional on the subject matter of the book or has competed extensive research in the field.
- The book is well-organized; the presentation of the material is systematic and flows well.
- The physical presentation is smart, engaging and professional-looking.

EDITING AND PROOFREADING

Editing and proofreading are two stages of the reviewing process for a manuscript. Though similar, they are different.

Editing begins as soon as the first draft is completed. Many writers will edit as they go along, stopping and editing the previous chapter or page. In editing, the draft is scrutinized for organization, transitions, flow, continuity, and evidential arguments.

A 'finished' book will always require making some cuts and changes. Do not be afraid to make major changes during editing and proofreading. The best books are those books in which the author can reject less than excellent writing. What the author views as his or her most excellent writing may be a bit too deep for the reader.

The last step in preparing the final draft is the proofreading. This phase is when the typographical errors, inaccurate or possibly misunderstood words or terminology, grammar problems, and punctuation errors are found and corrected. It should also be noted that good authors are not always good editors or proofreaders.

Once again, the scope of this book is not to get extremely embroiled in the book-writing process; however, for a publisher or author to know what to look for in a book as a possible project, the following editing essentials need to be considered:

- **The target audience.** If the book is a technical book or a DIY book, the vocabulary and instructions should be given in a way that the audience can understand.
- **Look at the sentences.** Wordy, clichéd, repetitive, and empty sentences should be avoided. Poor syntax will always be distracting to most readers and can destroy the credibility of even the most expert author.
- **Consider the words.** Personal and fiction works should use words which express a personal perspective and impression. Academic works should use more neutral vocabulary and less vivid descriptors.
- **Check grammatical details.** The work should maintain the same past or present tense throughout. Bad grammar is simply unacceptable in most written works with the exception of certain prose.
- **Spelling and punctuation must be impeccable.** Poor punctuation and spelling is another quick destroyer of a book's credibility.

Once a manuscript has boon completed, most authors will need a good editor and proofreader to assist in the final quality checks before starting the publishing process.

An eye-catching cover

As unfair as it might sound, books are judged by their covers and an unappealing book cover can keep a book from ever being sold in spite of the quality of its contents. Like the presentation of food in a fine dining-establishment influencing the perceived taste of the food, a book cover is a critical element of the reader's experience when choosing and enjoying a book. The cover is the first thing the reader sees. A great cover will draw in the potential reader; it will entice the reader to begin the journey of the book page by page. As the first thing seen by the reader, a great cover should draw the reader in; it should entice the reader to start discovering the words within the book, page by page.

EBooks are displayed on 'digital book shelves'. Readers, as they browse the web, click on cover images that appeal to them. These cover images are thumbnails and are small. These thumbnails allow for much less detail than the cover of a physical book. Appealing eBook covers must be designed with this thumbnail image in mind.

Creating an attention-grabbing, professional-looking cover that is appealing as a thumbnail image is not easy. If you do not have this talent, then you may want to find someone who can do this; ideally, contract with a graphic designer that has experience in creating eBook covers. But though eBook covers do have different characteristics than paper book covers, the eBook cover should not look out of place among paper book covers.

Choosing a self-publishing company

There is an ongoing debate about the current and future roles of paper books and eBooks. Rather than examine too deeply into that discussion, let's just look a few facts that both sides of the debate agree upon:

- Digital devices are here to stay
- People will be reading or listening to words on those devices in the foreseeable future
- No digital reading device has quite the physical options and utility as a paper book
- No eBook as quite the sensory appeal as a paper book
- It has become very easy and inexpensive to self-publish paper books and eBooks.

So, with these facts established, why not publish in both paper and digital formats?

There is a growing number of self-publishing companies (SPCs) vying for the opportunity to assist independent authors and publishers. As an independent author/publisher your first decision, after having a good manuscript in hand, is deciding whether to contract a SPC to do the editing, formatting, printing, and distributing of the book or if you will be taking care of these tasks yourself (actually doing the work yourself or hiring freelancers to do the work). Chances are you will want to mix the two strategies.

Most SPCs, for both POD and eBooks, will allow you to pick and choose what services you desire and need from them.

FINDING A SELF-PUBLISHING COMPANY

It can be very overwhelming to google self-publishing and to see the huge number of results for SPCs. There are literally dozens of such companies that offer hundreds of different self-publishing packages. These packages offer proofreading and editing, cover and content design, distribution, and marketing services. The prices can range from less than a hundred dollars to several thousands of dollars. SPCs will claim to be originated by certain genre authors for authors of that genre, to promote Christian or other cultural values, or have the contacts to promote your work in front of Hollywood agents.

To begin the weeding-out process to find the best SPC for you and your book you will want to answer the following questions:

- **What is the lowest price that you want to set for your book?** That may seem like a premature question due to the expenses of editing and design and formatting and print quality. Those expenses are important; however, they only matter if your book is competitively priced. Some SPCs maintain control over the price of your book. Sometimes their price is unrealistically high. The company may claim that the high-pricing increases potential royalties. However, royalties only occur when there are sales. An incredible book with great content, a beautiful cover design, and professionally editing is certainly desirable. But if the book is priced at $20 when there are other bestsellers on the same shelf or web page for $12 or less, the higher-priced book will not get nearly the sales volume. These SPCs that set high prices on self-published books are counting on the few dozen copies that the author/publisher will buy for family, friends, gifts, and promotional marketing to make their money. SPCs that will price your book out of the range of the competition should probably be avoided.

- **What is your, the author's, price for each copy of the book?** Many independent authors will be purchasing several dozen copies of the book as mentioned above. The more promotional work (i.e. reviewers, bloggers), book signings, lectures, speaking engagements, the more copies the author will want to buy and to have on hand to sell or give away. The author's price should be the actual cost of printing the book plus a 15-20% markup.

- **What royalties will you earn?** The SPC should make it easy to calculate royalties. Online royalty calculators are a part of most reputable SPCs web sites. These calculations will allow you to use different page sizes, paper quality, black and white or color interior, number of pages, and retail prices. If a SPC does not provide an easy method or calculator for determining royalties, the independent author/publisher should be suspicious. If any SPC states that potential royalties cannot be calculated without a reviewing the manuscript or having a formatted copy of the manuscript should be avoided.

- **Is the agreement exclusive or non-exclusive?** No SPSC should ask for or demand exclusive rights to a work. The SPSC has no reason to seek or to be given rights of the work in any other format or rights to movie, video, future editions or versions, or subsidiary rights. SPCs are not the same as traditional publishers that may have considerable capital invested in your book. They are only providing a service, have no investment, and are not entitled to any rights or options. Additionally, the contract should be easy to terminate by the author/publisher with 30 days' or less notice or the agreement should have a short-duration termination date. This termination option or short agreement period will allow for a traditional publisher to work with you should one become interested in your work.

- **Will the author/publisher receive production-ready files?** The SPC should provide final production digital files of the work. These files should be in MS Word or Adobe InDesign or another industry comparable format. Any SPC that will not provide such files after you have paid for the editing and design of the book should be avoided. It is your work. You paid them to do the task of putting the work into the file format. They are your files.

- **What is the SPC's reputation?** You will need to do some research apart from the company's website. The website Predators & Editors is a great place to begin checking on a company's history, operations, and reputation. Any and all companies will have some unhappy customers and detractors. When reading complaints, attempt to discover the legitimate ones. If there are multiple reports of unhappy customers, these should trigger some suspicion.

To self-publish electronically should be cost free once you have your manuscript and cover design. The best eBook SBCs and their platforms are free.

However, in order to be more competitive, many independent authors and publishers are choosing to invest in professional editing, book design, artistic covers, and marketing specialists. Professional freelancers in these areas are much less expensive than the often-times inflated prices that SPCs charge for the same services. But again, caution needs to be had when hiring freelancers.

MARKETING YOUR BOOK

In order sell any significant number of copies of your book, you will need to do some marketing in order let customers know about your book. Marketing your book might appear to be a daunting task but it does not have to be. You have already written a book; telling people about it should be much easier.

One of the more popular and effective ways to do this is by starting a blog or designing a web page in which you can share quality content of your book with readers and other bloggers and one in which you can directly promote your book. You can also write guest posts on other blogs to further expand your book and your blogs visibility. Asking for reviews from bloggers, reviewers, and other successful authors in the books genre is also a good tactic.

Other suggestions for marketing your book:

- **Have a marketing plan.** Attempt to stick to your plan but do not be afraid to improve the plan as you work it. When things change and an element of the plan is no longer pertinent, change that element. Your plan can be as detailed as you like, but it should have enough detail and thought so as not be ineffective. Simply stating that you will use online marketing is not a plan. The elements in the plan should also be able to be measured. You will want to gauge the effectiveness and performance of your marketing efforts. The significant point here is to be sure that you have a plan, that you can measure the performance of your marketing efforts as you go and that you know what your next step is.

- **Messaging and tone.** Much of a marketing message is not about the actual product being sold; rather much of the message is how you are selling the product. Wording, semantics, images, even fonts and colors, have a very big influence in how potential customers view your product. There is a reason why a ransom note looks and sounds different that an ad for chocolate ice cream. The challenge is to determine the best tone in the marketing message for your book. Not only are you attempting to differentiate you book from everyone else's book, but you want to give the potential readers a little bit of an idea of what they can expect in the book's pages. And pay attention to the tone of the message. When a dog takes a walk with its owner, the dog may not understand the words the owner is saying. However, the tone of the owner's words gives the dog a strong idea of what to expect in the next few moments. If your message and tone convey whimsical fun, then the reader will expect such. If the message and tone is classical elegance, then that will be expected.

- **Social Media.**
  - o Twitter's niche is authenticity and relationships. There is no need to open a new Twitter account to talk about your book unless you are using a *nom de plume*. Twitter can be used to connect with like authors and genre readers.
  - o Facebook is another good tool that, if it is done well, can create some interest and looks at your book. Many initial referrals and book sales come from family and friends; hence the Facebook connection. You may also want to create dedicated Facebook page for you book with a link from your personal page. Using Facebook, you can build excitement in the book before it is ever actually released leading to a bog rolling out promotion.
  - o LinkedIn is a powerful network for business and professional people. This makes it a good tool for non-fiction authors that have connections in their professional careers. A key thought here is that less is often more. People who are very busy do not like spam. If you send a

note to someone on LinkedIn, keep it short, concise, and do not send too many.

o Locate and connect with bloggers and review sites for your genre. Tell them about your book; provide them with copies to read. Ask the post their positive reviews. Some blogger may even offer to interview you. Other possible websites that you can use for exposure is Stumbleupon, Autharium, Blogtour, Bookroster, and Bookblogs.

o Pinterest is another site in which you can advertise your book. You pin the cover of your book with a description and a link to it in a board for potential readers to find.

o YouTube and Vimeo are the top video sites for social media. Many books can translate into a good video presentation. Having quality video that describes your book or a teaser offers a taste of its contents can spark a considerable amount of attention for potential readers.

• Email may be considered old-fashioned to many, but it still remains an effective communication channel for many people. Do not disregard using this forum to reach people. But when doing an email, do it carefully so that it is not seen as spam by the receiver or by the email servers. Produce an attractive, professional looking email that will entice the receiver to read the email's content.

- Selling the book is how income is made. Leading people to the web pages where your book is being sold is not the end. You have to provide an easy method for them to purchase the book. On retail sites such as Barnes and Noble and Amazon, prominence increases by sales rankings, reviews, and tags. Ask people who purchase the book from a retail site to leave an honest review. Of course good reviews are always nice, but mixed reviews are also helpful as readers will weigh the perceived good and the perceived bad of other readers. And a negative review or two among numerous positive reviews is not as damaging as you might think. Most readers have the discernment to know if a bad review is justified or legitimate.

- Offline marketing to local press, TV and radio is often an excellent way to get your book in front of very specific, targeted audiences. If the subject of your work is of local interest, use that interest as a marketing opportunity. People like to read of events, people, and places that are part of their daily lives.

- Change and repeat. Marketing has to be current and it has to be changing. Assess marketing tactics and strategies, make changes, and do it again. Try new ideas, designs, websites, and techniques.

Self-publishing a book, for good authors, is a popular and rewarding activity for many good reasons; and its providing an alternative income stream can also be a great benefit and additional reason to venture into that business realm.

BLOGGING

A weblog or blog is a dialog or informational site that is published through the Internet. A blog consists of posts or entries that discuss subjects and themes that are generic to the overall theme of that particular blog. Most blogs are the work of one individual or a small group of closely connected authors. However, multi-author blogs (MABs) are becoming more popular. MABs feature posts that are authored by large numbers of individuals. MABs are usually professionally edited and designed. Newspapers, media outlets, educational institutions, and advocacy groups are producing the increasing number of MABs.

The majority of blogs are interactive. They allow visitors to comment upon the posts. It is this interaction between the blogs' authors and the blogs' readers that distinguish them from static websites. This interaction places blogging in the realm of social networking.

Blogs may offer commentary on a specific subject; some may act as personal online diaries; other blogs provide online brand advertising of a specific individual, product, or company. Typically, a blog will combine information in the form of text and images and links to other web sites, blogs, or media related to the blog's theme and the post's subject matter. As mentioned, the readers' ability to comment is usually a vital part of blogging. While most blogs are focus upon text to convey information, some blogs focus on art, photography, video, music, and audio. Some blogs feature the microblogging of very short posts. Edublogs are often used as instructional tools and resources.

BLOGGING AS A BUSINESS AND INCOME STREAM

Bloggers aspire of creating a site in which thousands of daily readers visit the site, where thousands of readers visit each day, drink in the knowledge being presented, and leave comments of how their lives have been transformed and made whole by the words on this blog. Many of these same blogger envision having their blog earn them enough money that all they need to do is to write five hundred words a day three or four times a week and they will be able to travel to all of those exotic places that the "professional" bloggers speak of on their web sites.

But the first problem is that the first aspiration does not happen very often, at least not without putting considerable work into it. It is possible but it is not easy.

The second problem is that the second aspiration does not usually happen without some level of the first aspiration happening first.

GETTING STARTED

Universally, bloggers agree that monetizing a blog should not be the primary reason for beginning a blog; much like book sales should not be the primary reason for writing a book. You write on a blog because you desire to blog, not because you want to make money. (The one group of bloggers that disagree with this fundamental concept is those bloggers who make money from convincing potential bloggers to blog.) A blogger that is working to achieve a blog with a high readership will be a consistent blogger, will work to build an audience, and will work to lead new readers to their blog. A successful blog needs a specific focus; a unique perspective on the focus is a big advantage. Waking up one day and deciding to start a blog without having anything to say or having a reason to blog (outside of making money) is not how you start a successful blog.

A successful blogger will determine a target audience. If you are promoting your books, then you will want to attract potential readers and buyers of your book. Perhaps you are passionate about a cause, something political, societal, or cultural. If so, then your audience might be those who have or may have the same leanings and thoughts. After you have decided on your primary subject matter or theme and you have decided who your target audience is, you need to then conceive a focus, unique perspective, and begin to consider posts that will reach your target audience. Create a schedule of blogging and keep to it. The more frequently you blog the better for your blog and your audience; however, if you can only blog once or twice a week, then do that. The important thing is to stay with your schedule. Lastly, a successful blogger uses social media, contacts, friends and family, and other bloggers to create a reader base.

Those bloggers that have successfully turned their blogging into income streams have blogs that are very clear as to who they are designed to serve. The style of the side, the tone and message of the posts, the appearance of the site are all deliberate choices made to welcome the faithful blog followers. Keeping the flow of useful information, engaging dialogue and an easy to read and presentation are essential. The successful blogger knows what attracts that blog's followers and continually works to keep those followers and to attract those of like mind.

It is only after you have a growing following of readers and quality posts that a successful blogger begins to consider monetizing the blog.

MONETIZING STRATEGIES FOR BLOGS

There are several methods that top income-producing bloggers use to monetize their blogs. There are different techniques for the different niches that the blogs fit into.

ADVERTISING BANNERS

A web banner, or banner ad, is advertisement on a web page that is delivered to the page and serviced by a web ad server. The advertisement is imbedded onto the page. The ad has a link to the website of the advertiser. A code is also embedded into the ad tells the ad server from which web page the banner click was made. When a visitor to your blog clicks on a banner advertisement the click is recorded by the ad server indicating the click originated from web site. The web site owner can earn a commission and/or receive a percentage of any sales from the transaction that originated from that banner advertisement click.

However, to make any income from the banner ads the web site needs very large volume. Typically, a banner ad is only clicked after it has been viewed 500 times. If a sale is made by a quarter of the customers that go to a web site (a very optimistic estimation) then the web site or blog will need at least 1000 visitors a day just to earn any kind of commission from the banner ad placement.

Using banner ads is a bit precarious. Blog readers do not generally like bold advertisements. To maximize the effectiveness of banner ads choose merchant programs that are related to your blog or web site. And choose ads that match the voice and style of the blog.

CPM ADVERTISING

Cost per impression (CPI) or cost per mille (CPM) refers to the pay that a blog or web site receives each time that a banner ad is displayed on that web site. If your blog displays an ad for a merchant, that merchant compensates you each time someone sees that ad on your blog. The current rate of compensation for CPM advertising to web site owners is about $1 per 1000 impressions or views.

AFFILIATE SALES

Affiliate marketing is the promotion of another merchant's products and the earning of a commission from any sales due to your promotion activities. There are several different methods of creating affiliate sales that will bring income from your blog.

- **Promote products you use.** Followers of a blog generally have some level of trust in the blog. That can be a very positive point. Since they have some trust in you, they will be more willing to listen to you about a product that you are promoting. (But do not lose their trust by promoting products that could be problematic.)

- **Offer additional bonuses.** Bonuses are a common tool to boost online sales. Many times people will by a product because of the value of the attached bonuses. Usually, the products you promote on your blog will have an attached bonus. However, if you own a product you might want to sweeten the deal by offering one of your products. Attempt to bonus with products that have little to no cost for you such as an eBook or software program or app. Attach your bonus to their purchasing a product using your affiliate link.

- **Offer special coupons.** Product owners will usually generate unique, special coupon codes for their affiliates. Ask the product owner for such a coupon that you can place on your blog. Again, this method is showing your readers that you do care about them and want to help them save money.

- **Promote recurring payment products.** Some products such as club memberships and discount sales programs pay commissions each time the subscription is renewed. These are generally programs in which the members pay a monthly subscription. However, again be careful in what recurring products you are promoting. Promote products that are considered as necessities to the niche that you are blogging about. Promote quality products. The longer the member keeps the subscription, the longer you will receive commissions

- **Write product reviews.** The best way to generate sales from your blog is write product reviews. We mentioned the trust that your followers have in you. If you review a product and give them an honest appraisal of your experience of it, they will accept it. Each month, publish an in-depth review of an affiliated product that you have used. The review post should not be slanted towards selling the product. Make the review relevant to your readers. Tell them how you used and how they can use the product for their benefit. Show your readers how the product is helping you and they will be inclined to buy it if they can use it.

- **Showcase the tools you use.** Most tools that bloggers use have affiliate programs. We use software, plugins, web hosts, etc. We are happy with those products otherwise we would change. Tell your readers about your products. Recommend that they use your affiliate link to receive a good deal on the tool.

- **Promote products that offer big commissions.** This does not necessarily mean promoting products that offer 90% commission. It means promoting products with big ticket prices. The 10% commission on a $500 laptop computer is larger than the 90% commission on a $25 software package.

- **Invite product owners to write a feature for your blog.** No one has more expertise about a product than the product owner. A post about the product from the product creator will boost your credibility among your readers tremendously. And that product owner's post in conjunction with your honest review should generate a large number of sales of the product.
- **Google AdSense.** This is Google's advertising program that is designed to be content sensitive and targeted. Google's servers determine the theme of your blog and the subject matter of the posts. The servers then select ads based upon that content to place ads on your blog. Earnings are dependent upon impressions and number of clicks on the ads.

IS BLOGGING FOR AN INCOME STREAM WORTH THE TIME?

There are some professional bloggers that make many thousands of dollars per year. But the reality is that the vast majority of bloggers earn very little to nothing from their blogs. Close to half of all blogs earn less than $10 per month and that includes those with consistent new postings. Only 18% of bloggers earn more than $500 per month. Of those blogs in that percentage that make

$500 or more per month, nearly all of them have been around for five years or more. Almost no blog will receive any income in its first year of operation. And those bloggers who do earn more than $500 per month have three or more blogs brining in their income.[7, 8]

Now that you have some real numbers about possible income from blogging, you might want to consider a few more points that still provide some optimism for those who like to blog and want to blog.

Most bloggers have no intention of earning any income from their blogs. Any earnings are really an accident because these bloggers have done nothing to optimize or even to seek out any revenue streams. And of those bloggers that are attempting to monetize their blogs are new and their blogs are new.

Additionally, there are a whole lot of blogs that are simply pure junk and a waste of electrons. Really good, niche blogs that lots of people want to read are not that numerous. But those blogs that good, niche blogs are the type of blog that has the potential to earn current income and for that income to become more passive income.

---

[7] Pinola, Melanie. "Can I Really Make a Living by Blogging?" Lifehacker. March 6, 2014. Accessed September 16, 2014.
[8] Bullas, Jeff. "Blogging Statistics, Facts and Figures in 2012 - Infographic." Jeffbullass Blog RSS. 2014. Accessed September 16, 2014.

Making money from a blog will not be an easy task to begin with, but it can be done. Those who treat their blogs as a business, those who are disciplined and determined, and those who are patient will have a decent chance of surmounting the ever-increasing blogger crowd. Anyone can start a blog, but only the very serious can turn it into a business.

VIDEO BLOGGING

A video blog (vlog) is a collection of videos that is posted on a web site. The video can be those produced by the site owner or someone else. The web site can be owned by the person who owns the web site or the web site can be owned by another person or company. Video blogging is much like blogging but it is done using video as the primary means of communicating the author's message. Distribution of vlogs is the primary business of the YouTube and Vimeo platforms and web sites.

BLOGGING VS. VIDEO BLOGGING

First, the advantages and disadvantages of both:

BLOGGING:

Pros

- **Privacy.** Your physical image is not forever immortalized saying or doing something that you might regret.

- **More forgivable to errors.** Posts on a blog can be edited very quickly and easily.
- **Less expensive start-up.** A computer with an Internet connection is all the "store-bought" equipment needed to establish a good quality blog.
- **More durable.** Blogs lend themselves as to be used and read for extended periods of time. Bogs are also better for communicating hard pieces of information (i.e. graphs, statistics, and photos) for more academic purposes.

Cons

- **Requires more pure talent.** Writing descriptively is more difficult than showing a video of something. One's personality and thoughts is often more difficult to express on paper – no facial expressions, gesticulations, or body language.
- **More difficult for readers to identify with you.** Reading requires more effort from the audience than watching a video. Reading requires visualization of what the words are describing. Videos do that for you making it easier to "digest" what is being said. Readers are less likely to identify with you.
- **More competition.** Nearly a million blogs are being created worldwide a week and over half a million posts are written each day!

- **Audiences have increasingly shorter attention spans.** The need for immediate gratification and the lack of self-stimulated thought have come of age.

VLOGGING:

Pros

- **More personality.** Vloggers instantly creates a unique persona due to the presented demeanor and appearance.
- **Does not require good writing skills.** Some people simply do not have good writing skills. Vlogging allows these individuals to tell their story using a different format.
- **People like to people watch.** Vlogging allows people to do just that.

Cons

- **It involves public speaking.** Like writing, public speaking requires skills.
- **Unable to edit.** Once a video is posted, it cannot be edited. Annotations can be posted with the video; however, it is what is said in the video that people hear and see. A video can be deleted and reshot or edited, but any previous links to the original video will be broken.

- **Takes more time.** Vloggers say that it takes between four and eight hours to produce, edit, and post a typical video.

- **More costly.** While using the webcam on your computer or the camera on your cellphone is possible, these cameras do not usually produce quality video and audio recordings. To maximize the impact of your videos using a camcorder with a good lighting setup, microphone, tripod, and really good video editing tools are required.

- **A steeper learning curve.** Doing video is more difficult and technical and precise than working with the written word.

- **More difficult to produce a top video than a top blog.** A good video is dependent upon all the same factors as good blog plus a few. A good video is dependent upon a good script, good production, and good "acting".

- **Video hosting.** There are only two real options for placing your video on a web site that will have any exposure: Vimeo or YouTube. On either site you are able to take advantage of the huge traffic volume they produce. However, your content must comply with their rules. If it does not they will shut down the viewing of all your videos on your channel.

- **Vlogging is harder to monetize.** To receive revenue from YouTube you need an advertising partner. However, this function is not completely available for all countries just yet. The options to monetize a video are very similar to that of a blog; discreet ads are placed in the area around your video viewing screen. The key here is discreet and non-obtrusive; remember the site rules for YouTube and Vimeo. There is also the possibility of imbedding clickable ads within the video itself.

For most people, blogging is an easier and less expensive way to get their message out to the public. There does not appear to be any major difference in timelines. And they both require originality, effort, and constituency to make work. For most people who are looking for an alternative income stream with more passive income later, the traditional blog is probably recommended. However, for the person that has the tools, the talents, and the time, video blogging may open up a completely different customer group than you can be reached through traditional blogging.

HOW TO CREATE A VIDEO BLOG

1. **To start, you need a theme, a reason, or topic for your video blog.** There are many reasons for doing a video blog, but if you are looking to monetize the blog, then, like a traditional blog, you will need a niche target audience for best results.

2. **Next, locate a web host for your vlog.** There are several free services and hosts on the web though YouTube and Vimeo are the larger, more popular sites. You may even create a separate web page as you would a traditional blog, and then embed your videos onto your personal site.

3. **You need to name your vlog or channel.** You will also need to name each video. While content is more important than the name, the title should be catchy and easy to remember so that people can share the title with others and find it quickly on their return trips to the vlog or channel.

4. **Record and produce some content.** You will probably have some interest when people first discover your vlog or channel, but if you are not adding new content regularly, viewers will lose interest and cease to follow your site or channel. It is good to have several different videos ready to post, but post the videos according to a regular schedule, not all at once. It is better to post a couple weekly than to post a half dozen in a week and then nothing for the next several weeks.

5. **Post your videos.** When posting your videos you need to have good titles, good tags, and good descriptions for maximum search optimization.

6. **Collect other videos.** Look for other videos that will complement your videos and theme and post them to your site as permitted.

7. **Promote your vlog.** You have to let the world know that your site and channel and videos are available to be viewed! Search engine optimization (SEO), and simple self-promotion are the least expensive and often times the most effective ways of promoting a video blog.

8. **Monetize the video blog.** Depending upon the rules of who is hosting your site and videos, and the content, you may be able to make some money.

CHAPTER FOUR

ALTERNATIVE INCOME STREAMS THAT REQUIRE HIGHER CAPITAL INVESTMENT

The goal of having income streams should include the ability of that stream to eventually generate more passive income. In simple terms, passive income will flow into your checking account whether or not you work that particular day or not. Some of the more common sources of the more passive income streams are stock dividends, bond interest, royalties and licensing income from patents and copyrights, payments from annuities, and rents from real estate properties. These favored passive income sources also require higher capital investment.

WHAT TO LOOK FOR IN HIGHER INVESTMENT INCOME STREAMS

Due to the fact that considerable capital investment is required to initiate these type alternative income streams, they should be scrutinized using a different set of criteria than other potential income streams. Before adding a high capital investment alternative income stream to your portfolio, look at and evaluate four important traits:

- **Security of the income stream.** The greater the investment the more security the investment should offer. This is even more important for the passive income stream investment. Few of us can afford to lose great amounts of cash and we want to be assured that the passive income from the investment will continue.

- **Growth of passive income generated.** Excellent investments become more valuable as time passes. This is because the core business or property that is generating the income is and will increase in value at a rate higher than inflation. The idea is to invest some cash into something. That something will begin to pay you some money. Excellent investments will pay more for the same investment in the future than it pays now. Stocks in growing companies and real estate properties which appreciate are examples of this.

- **Diversification of the core assets.** If an income stream is to do nothing more than produce an income, then all that matters is how many dollars the stream produces. Thus, if all things are equal, it is better to have $50,000 a year income from fifty different core assets that each produces a $1000 annually than to only have two core assets producing $25,000 annually. In the latter case, the loss of income from just one core asset will cause a catastrophic decrease in your income. If you are in a time of life in which you are using the passive income to live, your lifestyle just changed for the worse in a very big way.

- **Tax consequences.** Taxes are something that should be considered with great thought especially if the income stream is to be used for living expenses. To focus on the amount of money an investment earns without considering the amount of that money you actually can keep is simply fool hearted if that money is needed for living. Not all passive income is treated or taxed the same. Some corporate stocks dividends are taxed on one rate while distributions from partnerships are taxed in another manner. Some municipal bonds pay interest that is tax free while traditional bond interest can be taxed at rates nearing 50%. This great disparity in tax laws can be a boost or it can be a problem for passive income streams.

REAL ESTATE AS AN INCOME STREAM

Developing an income stream with real estate has traditionally been a safe investment with good future passive income. This security is even greater if the properties are in residential rental properties. Like all things that have or produce value, in real estate investing there is some work involved and there is some knowledge to acquire to accompany the capital asset investment.

Obviously real estate is a more expensive strategy in developing a passive income, but it is also one of the quickest strategies in seeing a return. Self-publishing and blogging take a longer time to see a return on the time and effort invested, whereas purchasing a rental property may have an income within thirty days after close. Each type of real estate property has advantages and disadvantages in owning. You will need to determine which is best for you at the moment before you make you purchase.

STEPS TO BUILDING A REAL ESTATE INCOME STREAM

1. The first thing to do is set an income goal. This number does not need to be the total figure that you must need to survive. This figure will probably serve better to be thought of as a smaller, reasonable amount of money that you would like to put into your from your investment of capital and time and effort.

2. Determine how much capital that you are willing to invest into the first property. Use that number as the base to calculate the value of the property that you can purchase. Things that you will need to pay for with that initial investment include the down payment, legal fees, closing costs, taxes due, insurance, the first month's mortgage loan

payment, and any repairs and alterations that may need to be made before renting or reselling the property.

3. Once you have determined the price range of the properties to look for, begin your search. As mentioned, residential real estate property is probably the surest and best property type for a beginning investor. The following section discusses what to look for in choosing good rental property for investment.

4. After choosing possible properties, you will need to determine if the costs of ownership of the property plus the cost of the loan payment plus any management fees subtracted from the possible rental income will be enough in the positive reach the income goal you have established. When looking at the cost of ownership, you will need to include taxes, insurance, maintenance and repairs, and upgrades need to keep it or increase its value. Will you be managing the property or will you have a hired property manager? You should also consider vacancy time. Very rarely is rental property occupied by a tenet 100% of the time. When one tenet moves out there will invariably be some time before the next tenet moves in. All of these expenses plus the amount of unpaid

rents must be taken out of the potential rental income.

5. Make an offer to purchase the property. You will usually want to place an offer lower than the asking price as nearly all list prices are set with negotiating room included. You can always go up on an offer, but you can never go down from a previous offer. Properties that have been on the market for a longer time are often good targets for low offers. Properties that are in bad condition or in which the owner is motivated to sell are also good properties to purchase at less than list price. If your offer is rejected, you may wish to make another offer, but take your time. Negotiating on a price can take some time in most markets. That being noted, if your numbers are good and the property is one that will make a good investment and income, then you may want to make good offer to begin with.

6. Complete the purchase. This will involve some legal matters that you may want to have an attorney or someone else that is very familiar with real estate contracts, mortgages, deeds, and real estate transitions to assist you before you sign the final documents. And before you make a deposit, talk with the owner to discuss potential problems. You may want to have a third party inspector to go over the property. Depending

upon the jurisdiction and loan procedures, it may take thirty to sixty days to close the transaction. If a property owner does not allow an inspection before a deposit, look elsewhere.

7. Once you own the property you will need to start managing the property or to hire a property manager. Getting the property ready for tenets, marketing the property for rent, showing the property to prospective tenets, dealing with lease contracts, collecting the rents, and seeing to repairs and maintenance takes time. A good property manager is usually available at affordable rates. If you decide that you are in a place to do these things, then you will need to determine if it is an economically good choice for you to manage the property or if your time would be better utilized working on another project.

8. Continuing work. Once the property is rented, the income does take on a more passive character; however, that does not mean that things are now completely hands-off. You will inevitably have some bad tenets, expensive repairs, and not-so-good repair technicians and contractors. You will have to make some decisions to keep the income flowing as smoothly as possible.

CONSIDERATIONS IN SEARCHING FOR RESIDENTIAL RENTAL PROPERTY

STARTING YOUR SEARCH

Having a real estate agent to assist you in the completion of a real estate purchase may be something to consider. However, you should start you search without one. Remember, real estate agents want you to buy at a premium price and to buy quickly. Neither of these things is conducive to the maximum profit or income stream possible in your buying the property. Real estate agents can and often create undue pressure and can sometimes sours a negotiation with suggestions that are in the agent's favor rather than the buyer's or the seller's best interests. The best approach to take in looking at properties for rental income is one that is unbiased and concentrates upon the business side of things. Look at all properties that are in the geographic area you have chosen that are within your price range. Just because you have $10,000 to invest does not mean that you have to use that entire amount on this particular purchase. The goal is to establish multiple, diverse core assets in your real estate passive income stream.

Also remember that you investing and price range is dependent upon whether you will have a property manager or if you will be a landlord that takes care of all the marketing, the maintenance, and the managing of the property. If you are the landlord, you will want to limit your search to areas that are close to your residence.

NEIGHBOURHOODS

The quality of the neighborhood is the primary consideration for most rental tenets. The type and condition of the neighborhood will influence the type of tenet that is attracted to the property and the type neighborhood will influence your vacancy rate. If the neighborhood is near a university, then it is likely that your tenets will be students. While rental prices may be higher in the neighborhood, you will probably have higher vacancy rates.

PROPERTY TAXES

Property taxes are not equal even within the same town. Before you can determine what your net income from owning and renting the property will be you must know what the property tax cost is. High property taxes are not always detrimental. Neighborhoods that are attractive to long-term tenets and that can command higher rents are often in higher taxed areas. But the opposite also exists; there are neighborhoods in which attempting to find a good tenet is an impossible chore and will still have high property taxes. Tax information is public information and you should be able find how much annual taxes are on piece of property very easily.

SCHOOLS

Tenants will often have children or will be planning to have children. Most parents are very concerned about the schools their children will attend. Residential properties that are located in higher rated school districts or are located near higher rated individual schools are often better investments due to the type of tenets that are attracted to these properties. While the school district or proximity of a school may not affect the immediate rental income, properties in poorly rated school districts or that are located considerable distances from schools often have lower resell prices.

CRIME

Nobody desires to live in a neighborhood that is a high crime zone. Talk to the neighbors of the property about crime in the area. Check with the police for vandalism rates (these crimes affect your repair costs) as well as burglary and more serious crime rates in the neighborhood. Look to see if the crime rates in the area and nearby neighborhoods are increasing or decreasing. Ask about the frequency of police patrols passing through the neighborhood. Rental properties in high crime neighborhoods typically have higher vacancy rates.

JOBS

Those areas that have opportunities for people to work are more attractive to tenets. People will move into these areas seeking work and people who have work need places to live. Check web sites for employment rates and job statistics for the area. Notice if any new corporations are moving into the area. However, new corporations in area can also have negative effects upon real estate values. Ask yourself if this is a corporation that you would not mind living in close proximity to. Your answer will likely mirror that of possible tenets.

AMENITIES

Look at the neighborhood for current or projected transportation, shipping, malls, gyms, parks, theaters, and other neighborhood perks that attract tenets. Visit city and community web sites to get an idea of where a good blend of public amenities and residential properties are located.

BUILDING PERMITS AND FUTURE DEVELOPMENT

Find out what is planned for the area in the few years. The local or municipal or county zoning commission or planning department will have information on any proposed or scheduled construction as well as changes to zoning areas. If new schools, condominiums, apartments, or shopping malls are scheduled, the area is probably growing. New industrial areas that will cause the loss of green space, or coming industries that are unattractive to residential areas could be potential problems. New apartments or condos could also become competition for tenets.

AMOUNT OF LISTINGS AND VACANCIES

Drive through the area and look online and in newspapers to get an idea of the amount of listings of rental houses in the area. An unusually large number of listings in or within a close proximity of the neighborhood could be an indication of a seasonal flux or that the neighborhood has become attractive to tenets. You will need to determine the cause for the high number of rental valances before buying. If the vacancies are seasonal, will they be tolerable due to higher rents when they are rented? Large numbers of listings and high vacancy rates cause property owners to lower rents. Low vacancy rates will allow for increased rental rates.

RENTS

Rental rates are where your income streams come from. You will need to have a very good idea of the amount of rent you can expect from a property. If the rent earned will not cover the loan payment, taxes, and all the other expenses, you should continue your search. You will need to assess the area and the property well enough to have a good idea of what rental income should be for the next five years. Affording the property now is good, but will the property need a new roof in the next three to four years? Is the automobile assembly plant that is the county's largest employer starting to lay off workers?

NATURAL DISASTERS

As you will have insurance on the property and will be considering that expense, you will need to get a very good idea of how much insurance and the type you will need. Not every insurance policy will cover every type of natural disaster. Flood prone areas require special flood insurance. Property insurance in areas prone to hurricanes or earthquakes needs to be diligently and carefully scrutinized to assure that a loss will be tolerable. Will the insurance cover rebuilding and loss of rents? The monthly premium on some policies will eat away any rental income.

GETTING INFORMATION

Renters in the neighborhood and homeowners will be good sources of information. Talk to those folks. Renters are much more honest about the negative aspects of the area than the homeowners are as the homeowners have an investment and this is their permanent home. If you settle upon a particular neighborhood, attempt to visit the area at different times on different days of the week. Doing so will give you a better overall idea of what to expect as well as giving you different people to visit with.

THE PHYSICAL PROPERTY

Residential rental property can be single-family dwellings or multi-family dwellings. Duplexes and condominiums can also make good first rental properties as an investment. Condos can be a good choice as the condo association will assist with external repairs. But there are the condo association fees that must be paid. And condo owners really only own and have limited control over the interior of the condo. And as condos are not independent living units, their rents are usually lower and their value appreciates less quickly.

Single-family dwellings usually attract longer-term tenets more so than condos. Families and couples are usually more financially stable, can pay the rent, and are less mobile than single-person tenets. The simple fact is that two can live almost a cheaply as one when considering rent, utilities, and food. The additional income provides more stability. As a potential rental property owner you will want to find properties that are attractive to this type of tenet.

When you have narrowed your search down to a particular area, you should seek properties that have the potential to appreciate as well as having a good cash flow projection. You may want to look at properties that are just a bit over your price range as well as below your maximum price. Some properties are priced very high but an offer for a lesser amount may still purchase the property. Watch the listing prices of properties that do sell and ask the buyers what the final sale price was. This will give you an idea of what market value for the neighborhood is. New buyers may also be good sources of other useful information. For maximum appreciation value, look for properties that with a few cosmetic changes and minor renovations, will attract those tenets that can afford higher rents. These cosmetic changes and renovations will increase the resell value if you decide to sell it in a few years.

THE BOTTOM LINE

Nothing is assured. You will have to make a calculated and informed estimation for your projected cash flows. You can never be completely sure about tenets. Nature is nature and people are people; there will always be some unpredictability to live with. Every city and town and community and neighborhood has its good properties. However, it takes some work and research to find those properties. Once you have located the ideal property, maintain realistic expectations. Assure that your personal finances are healthy.

Remember that if might be a couple of months before the first rent check is deposited into your checking account; not having some cash to cover the first couple of mortgage payments can really create some major financial stress. Also, real estate investing does not begin with buying a rental property. Rather, it begins

with your having created the financial situation that
enables you to buy a rental property.

CHAPTER FIVE

STARTING YOUR OWN BUSINESS

Dear Business Coach,

I have become tired of the daily grind of working for someone else according to their rules, the schedule, and their ideas. I have begun dreaming of starting my own business. I have heard so many good things about being your own boss and I think that I would like to try it. However, this is something that I have never done before and I am a bit worried about failing. Is there a way to know if starting my own business is really a good idea or if I should simply stay in the grinder?

Signed,

Smitten with Working for Self

******

Dear Smitten,

Beginning your own business could be the best career move you might ever make; a decision that may lead to big rewards, control over your own destiny, and personal independence. Hundreds of thousands of new businesses are being started every month. But running and starting a business is not only challenging, it is also involves risk. Therefore, before investing considerable time, time that you can never get back, and investing your life's savings, which is becoming more difficult to recoup once lost, you should be fully aware and understanding of what is needed to be a successful business owner.

Do not worry that you may not have an MBA or have several years of business experience. If you have the ability to do some research and can learn from that research, and if you know yourself and can give an honest appraisal of your strengths, weaknesses, talents, and inabilities (yes, inabilities), then you can make this important decision. Here are some things that you need to contemplate before you make the jump from employee to entrepreneur.

LET'S LOOK AT THE PROS AND CONS OF OWNING A BUSINESS.

We need to do this so that we can answer the first big question: do the benefits of owning your own business outweigh the disadvantages?

Pros

The pros are reasonably obvious. They are the reason millions of people, like you, envision quitting their conventional jobs. Your reasons for beginning your own business should not be solely for the financial opportunities. Some of the following pros should also be included in your personal list of reasons for starting your business:

- You do what interests you, perhaps even what you love doing, and you are making a living doing it
- You are in control, at least to a large degree, of when you work, where you work, and with whom you are work
- You are able to choose you clients, your projects, and what other businesses you will buy from or partner with
- You can find a work/life balance that is tailored to your life situation and family
- You may work more efficiently since you will be free from office politics and bureaucracy
- You may have a chance to earn more money than you did before (but it is okay if you do not)
- You will have greater job security (business owners have more than one customer, employees only have one customer – their employer
- You get to create your own something
- You have a personal life purpose in the morning and a wonderful sense of accomplishment at the end of the day

Cons

But there is always a list of disadvantages to every decision. Would any of the following disadvantages create major troubles or be extremely stressful for you?

- You will be dealing with an uncertain income and a fluctuating cash flow (some weeks you may get paid really good, some weeks you do not get paid)

- Finances and tax reporting will be much more complicated
- Banks, credit card companies, and other lending institutions will require you to meet a higher criteria for their services
- You must be a self-starter with extreme amounts of determination every day you wake up
- You will be responsible for and doing everything needed to run the business, i.e. paperwork, accounting, finances, marketing, selling, delivering, legal matters, collecting from nonpaying clients, purchasing materials and supplies, cleaning the office bathroom
- If you want the paid benefits that you may have received as an employee, you have to pay for them and they are usually expensive, i.e. health insurance and vacation time (for business owns there is no such thing as paid time off)
- You will probably be working more total hours
- You may experience problems such as loneliness, isolation, and depression due to working without people around you
- The combined stress of all these cons could be greater than the stress of working as an employee

Yes, there are a lot of disadvantages to owning your own business. However, nearly all of the disadvantages can be overcome or minimized. Finances and irregular cash flow can be managed by strategic budgeting. Affordable insurance options are available for many people. You can set your rates and prices to account for time off.

EVERY SUCCESSFUL BUSINESS HAS A GOOD IDEA AND A MARKET. DO YOU HAVE ONE?

If the above reality check has not completely changed your mind about starting your own business, then that is great sign. There is a good chance that you may have the fortitude and tenacity that business owners need. However, resolve is not everything you will need to get started. You will also need a good idea and you will need to find people that can and will buy your idea.

Is your idea a good one? A good business idea does not have to be a ground-shaking, mind-blowing, unique idea. A good business idea just has to be one that a profitable business can be structured around. It can actually be someone else's idea that you are using in a different way, in a different location, or with a different clientele. There is no reason to look for the meaning of your life and attempt to monetize that meaning. You do not have to wait until a revolutionary epiphany strikes you. Many business ideas that have become revolutionary trends began as a different take or perspective on an old idea. The international company AirBNB was started in 2008 as a takeoff from travel web sites. The three cofounders of the company found a niche and reworked the travel web site idea into their niche. AirBNB has now become a serious threat to the competing hotel industry.[9]

We have no real way of knowing what business idea will be the next business model that will take the world by storm until after the first customers have used the idea and begin telling their friends about it.

Discuss your business idea with friends, Facebook, family and strangers. The most important thing is not if you think the idea is a good one, rather the important things is do other people think the idea is a good one. We need to have confidence in our idea, but self-confidence is one thing, but confidence based upon the words of others will sometimes go farther.

Is there a market for your idea? Perhaps a better question is: Will people actually purchase your idea? If so, who are these people and where are they? Test your idea by offering it to some potential customers for their reaction. Did they offer to buy it? What were their thoughts about the price and the usage of the product? Design a small website and send it the link to some people for their reaction to the product, the site, and the pricing of the product.

There are a few excellent and free market research tools available to determine if your business idea is something that people are interested in and desire. Google's

---

[9] Harpaz, Joe. *Airbnb Disrupts Hotel Economy, Sends Regulators Scrambling*. Forbes. May 7, 2014. Accessed September 18, 2014.

KeyWord Tool, Google Insights, and Google Search can be used to look for trends relating to your idea. You can also do a quick survey of possible competition. Government data bases, such as those for census information, small business information, and commerce information, may also offer good information towards potential customers and competition.

If you have a business idea that is something people will buy, then you have the primary ingredients for a successful business. Just a few dollars, you may be able to start your own business.

SHOULD I START MY OWN BUSINESS?

After you have completed an early assessment of your business idea and have concluded that there could be a market for it, then you will want to develop a business plan. (We talked about business plans in a previous chapter). While you are working on the business plan you will also want to do some very important personal assessing. While the business plan will look at the logistical details needed to bring your idea to fruition, you will also need to determine if you have the entrepreneurial spirit and mindset required to build a successful business.

Many academic studies have been conducted over the past three or so decades looking to identify the characteristics, traits and behaviors that set successful entrepreneurs apart from the unsuccessful ones. MIT's professor, Jeffrey Timmons identified several inherent personal traits and personal behaviors that successful entrepreneurs need to possess[10]:

- Self-confidence
- Drive and energy
- Internal control of focus
- High levels of personal responsibility and initiative
- Little fear of failure
- Tolerant of ambiguity
- Willing to commit to long-term
- Moderate risk taker
- Able to make use of criticism and feedback
- Sees money as a tool or a measure rather than as an end goal
- Able to maximize resources
- Continual and pragmatic in problem solving
- Sets clear goals
- Self-imposes standards

The qualities (i.e. drive and energy and self-confident) are intrinsic. Either you have them or you do not. They can be developed but in most people developing them to such a degree that they influence behavior without conscious thought requires longer periods of time. The behaviors can usually be developed more quickly and most of will need some development of these behaviors. However, the more of these behaviors and characteristic that you have at to begin with, the easier, the quicker,

---

[10] Timmons, Jeffry A. *The Entrepreneurial Mind*. Andover, Mass.: Brick House Pub., 1989.

and the more effective it will be for you to overcome all of the "cons" to owning a business.

It is important that you be very honest with yourself when thinking about your capabilities, your behaviors, and your weaknesses. If you are someone that tends to be disorganized, forgetful of deadlines, or have a hard time motivating yourself to do things you do not like doing, beginning or owning your own business probably is not right for you.

Years ago, my first business was selling insurance. I made a living at it. However, the business never grew. I simply did not like doing sales work. Twenty years later, I tried sales again; this time in insurance and securities. Again, I made some money, but I still was not cut out to do sales. However, I have been fortunate to have other skills, talents, and knowledge that I have been able to market and sell. I learned the importance of honestly appraising what I am able to put into a business and what I am willing to put into a business. And sometimes the two are vastly different.

START SMALL

You do not have to start your business on a huge scale. Most successful businesses start off as part-time ventures in someone's basement, garage, or spare bedroom. Occasionally, your regular job might allow you to use some of your extra time to work on your own business. You will also need to remember that working full-time and putting in a lot of hours in your own business can be exhausting. Chances are that after you have grown a cash reserve equal of a couple years' salary or once you have several steady clients or numerous customers, are at the point where you move into your personal business full-time. It is likely that your full-time attentions will create even more and quicker success in the business. Lastly, you will need to know how you will deal with the difficult times. You will also need to know when it is time to cease a particular venture. Having a passion for the business that you are starting is what pushes you through those difficult times. However, uncontrolled passion can also be the route to unneeded heartache. We have to recognize and seek balance in all things. Be realistic and do some planning for possible failures. A significant number of new businesses do fail (usually due to poor management, poor planning, or not a good idea to begin with). However, failure can still lead to success. Nearly all highly successful entrepreneurs have had at least one business failure.

Hopefully, with the above insights, thoughts, and suggestions you will be able to decide if starting a business is right for you. If you do decide to go forward, perhaps some of this information will help you to set up your business for success.

Cheers,

Business Coach

START YOUR OWN SMALL BUSINESS

If you have decided that your starting your own small business is a good thing for you to do and you are ready to start the business, then it is time to actually start the start-up.

CREATING THE CONCEPT

As we talked about, potential entrepreneurs must have a good idea that is ready to or already is generating a steady income before quitting their regular job. This is not easy. There should be a plan that uses the entrepreneur's knowledge, expertise, and experience in a way that allows for the greatest amount of income.

Your primary business ideas should come from those areas in which you currently have considerable interest, knowledge of, and have the materials and equipment necessary to start the business. This will keep the start-up costs lower and will allow you start right away. The knowledge will give you an advantage over competition that lacks your knowledge. Your interest will make it easier to keep working when distractions arise.

But doing something that you enjoy doing is not the only consideration. You must be able to market and to sell what you are doing. If the business does not have a market to sell to or if there is not enough money in the selling of the product or service, you need to find another idea.

DEVELOPING A WORK SPACE

Most people's homes are where most small businesses get started. However, the home is designed to be lived in. Every house is not conducive to just any type of home business. If you are looking at doing some sort of manufacturing business, be sure that you shed or garage is large enough for you working there without forcing your vehicle and family's belongings into wind, rain, snow, or heat. The same thought goes for using the spare bedroom or den or dining room table. There will undoubtedly be inconvenience with running a home business from home, but you need to make sure that the inconvenience is manageable.

If you work is will be Internet or computer based, you will need to assure that your hardware and software technology is of a level needed to do the work. Check your band width and speeds for your Internet service provider. You may need to upgrade your service. You will probably want to have some privacy for your office if you are communicating with customers. A barking dog or a crying baby may not only be distracting, it could be detrimental to a sale. Customers like to think that they are the most important consideration you have at the moment that you are talking with them.

OUTSOURCING PARTNERS OR EMPLOYEES

Yes, it is good to be the singular owner of a small business and to have complete control over that business. However, there are times when needing additional funds, knowledge, or experience requires that a business partnership be formed. When choosing a business partner, look for someone who will represent your company the way that you want it represented. In addition to bringing the required resource that you are seeking, what other advantages and benefits will the partner bring to the business? Is the potential partner bringing some unwanted history or traits or behavior that will be detrimental to the business? Will you look forward to working with this person on a regular basis?

Attempt to outline, define, and designate the tasks that all partners will be responsible for. This will keep disagreements fewer, reduce confusion, and allow for performance to be more easily measured. You will also need to keep the legal contracts, licenses, statutes of corporation or partnership, and other legal paperwork current. Refilling some papers may be required, but keeping things current and legal is the best way to operate and to prevent future problems.

You will also want to determine if you will be hiring employees now or possibly in the future. If it is remotely possible that you will need employees, then you will want to consider things like payroll and accounting now so that there will be no problems when or if you do hire them. You will also need to consider from where those employees will work. Will you want them to have unfettered access to your garage or home?

DOING YOUR RESEARCH

There are many books and web sites – most written by people whose business is to sell you something for your business – that will tell that after coming up with an idea to "just go for it" and to "jump right into the deep end". These are bold approaches that may work occasionally; however, these approaches can also create some unintended, consequences.

A probable better move is talk with people about the business idea and to show them your business plan. When having these conversations, ask them some specific questions:

- Would you buy this particular product?
- How much do you think it is worth? How much would you pay for it?
- How would you market the idea or product?
- Do you think this will be a long-term product that people would want and use in the future or would you call it a fad-thing?
- How would you improve the idea or product?
- Do you know of other businesses that are doing this or selling this product? What do you think of their idea or service or product?

For those who have family that you are responsible for, you should be talking to those family members about their feelings of the business. If they live with you, they will be inconvenienced just as you are. If they enjoy your time with them, what do they think about possibly having less time with you? Do they understand that the family financial situation may also change? If you get some negative comments from the family, you will need to devote some time in discussing and evaluating those concerns. You will likely need to find some compromises. You may need to decide if your personal goal is worth pursuing against a family member's wishes.

Once you have talked with friends, family, and strangers about your business idea and plan, then it is time to review and modify your idea and plans. You will have likely discovered ways to improve the product, its production process, its marketing, or the administration side of the business. Modify your plans to include these improvements or to show them as options. It is these improvements that will likely be the distinguishing feature that separates your product and idea from the competition.

FINDING FUNDING

Now that you have a refined, definite, workable plan and you have the support of the family, you will want to secure funding. Most businesses require some startup capital. A good goal is that you will be able to recoup your initial investment within a year. However, keep in mind that even successful businesses may operate in a deficit for a couple of years. Different sources of funding that may consider are:

- Small-business loan

- Savings
- Money generated from other income streams
- Family/friends as investors
- Personal loan from lending institution
- Home equity loan

You might note that I did not include credit cards on the above list. This is not an oversight. With most economies having very little growth, at least at the street level, and with credit card interest rates so high, their use as a funding tool should be completely avoided. Also, avoid borrowing from or against retirement plans.

You should also build upon an emergency fund before you go full-time into your business. Having three months of living expenses in an account will remove a lot of stress and allow you to spend your efforts and time on the business.

COVERING YOUR BASES

Business owners need to think about the possibility of health or other issues that cause the income streams or the business to cease. If a partner becomes unable to work, who would take over the business? If you become disabled, is there a backup plan for taking care of the monthly expenses?

LOOKING INTO THE FUTURE

It is good to own your own business. But at some point, the entrepreneur will probably have a desire to retire or to move to on other interests or another business. Your business plan should eventually include the transferring or selling or closing of the business. If your business depends solely upon your unique knowledge or skills, then it may not be able to be sold. Thinking of such a business as a retirement source or source for future investments may not be applicable.

There are very few things that are as rewarding and as satisfying as starting, developing, and owning your own business. However, a successful ending comes after lots of work and planning before the first dollar is ever received from that first customer.

CHAPTER SIX

A FEW WORDS ABOUT...

Before any person can expect to be successful in any business, either as an employee or as a business owner, that person must have some basic and general knowledge, some skills, and some values about how to live within a culture and society. These same skills, knowledge and values will usually translate and crossover into our business lives, our family lives, and our very personal lives that no one but us, the individual, sees and experiences. Hence, reference material such as this book, would be amiss and negligent not to mention at least the most fundamental of these common skills, knowledge, and values that will affect each of us every day, every waking minute, no matter what we are doing.

...PERSONAL FINANCE & BUDGETING

Unfortunately, personal finance is not a mandated course in high school or college; therefore it is common to find young people that when stepping out into the real world for the first time to be completely clueless when it comes to managing their money. Understanding personal finance is really very easy and there is no good reason for any individual not to have some knowledge of

No successful business has ever operated without having a budget.

the subject. If someone can read a Facebook page, that person can gain some knowledge of personal finance. Good math skill are not even required if you can download an app to your telephone.

For those of you who desire to live a comfortable and efficacious life, let's take a look at seven extremely important financial concepts. While these cannot guarantee wealth and prosperity and happiness, it is extremely hard to have a life of wealth, prosperity, and happiness without practicing these eight concepts.

LEARN SELF CONTROL

If you are fortunate, your parents instilled this skill and trait in you as you were growing up. If they did not, then understand that the quicker you learn that instant gratification is destructive, the quicker you will find yourself with your finances in order. Although it is possible for you to effortlessly swipe a credit card and take home a pair of new prewashed, pre-torn, pre-worn out skinny jeans or to charge the newest iPhone that pretty much does the same things as the perfectly good iPhone that you have in your pocket, ask yourself if they are needed. Are they really worth the several hours of work that is required to pay for them? Do you really want pay interest, interest equal to an extra hour of work every week for a year, on those jeans or iPhone? If you make a habit of putting everything on your credit card without paying off the balance every month, you may well find yourself paying for that iPhone and those jeans for several years after they have been tossed into the dumpster. Using your credit card for the convenience factor or the rewards they offer is fine so long as you pay the balance every month. And do not carry more credit cards than you can manage. There really is no reason to have more than two cards for most people.

ASSUME CONTROL OF YOUR FINANCIAL FUTURE

If you do not learn to handle you own money, other people will mishandle your money for you. Some of those people are actively trying to take what little money you have left away from you. The Internet is teaming with unscrupulous financial planners, bill consolidators, and credit counselors who will charge incredible fees to do exactly what you can do. Other people may have good intentions but may have even less financial knowledge than you have; like grandma who wants you to buy a house near her even though you can only afford an adjustable-rate mortgage with a huge balloon read a few basic books on personal finance. When you have some basic knowledge you will be prepared to ask better questions about using, saving, spending, and growing your money.

KNOW WHERE YOUR MONEY GOES

Once you have read through just a couple of personal finance books, you will understand the importance of not spending more than you earn. This is best accomplished by budgeting. Once you see how much you spend on your pack-a-day cigarette habit or your daily Starbucks coffee over the course of a month, you will realize how adjusting everyday expenses can have as much an effect on your financial situation as a raise in salary. And by keeping recurring monthly expenses low you will be able to save more money over time. Rather than spending your money on a posh apartment now, save for a few years and then buy a nice condo or house.

START AN EMERGENCY FUND

"Pay yourself first." Yes, you may have student loans and credit card debt that you have to pay. However, if you do not have an emergency fund with $100 in it, the next time you have an ear infection you will be increasing your debt and the interest on that doctor's visit and bottle of antibiotics. You need to put back something – any amount – on a regular basis as part of your budget. Having money for those small emergencies can keep you out of financial trouble. If you begin the habit of seeing this emergency fund payment as non-negotiable, you will find it easier to save for retirement or vacations or a down payment on a house.

Don't put your emergency fund somewhere easily accessible. Put into an interest-earning savings account. This will make it more inaccessible for those moments of weakness and it will help to keep inflation from eroding the value of your savings.

START SAVING FOR RETIREMENT NOW

Have you heard of compound interest? You will when you read those personal finance books. Compound interest is what allows you to have large retirement accounts in thirty years with seemingly small monthly contributions. But because of the way it works, you need to start that saving as soon as possible. The longer you save, the better compound interest works. If you start soon enough in saving for retirement you may find yourself seeing work as option rather than as a necessity before you are start getting senior citizen discounts. The other thing to consider is that employers will often match cash employees' contributions into retirement programs. You will also find some tax advantages to saving for retirement now rather than later.

GET A GRIP ON TAXES

The subject of taxes is not always an easy subject to understand, but it is one that you will need some knowledge of as soon as possible. If a company offers you a salary or when you are looking for work, you should understand how to calculate if your take-home check will cover you monthly expenses and financial goals. Your take-home check is very dependent upon your withholding taxes. Fortunately, there are many online paycheck calculators that will give you a very accurate estimation of your net pay after deductions. And as each jurisdiction and city has very different tax rates, you will need to consider each job offer differently. One other thing about taxes; the higher your salary, the higher your withholding tax rate is. For example, if your current salary is $35,000 per year and you get an increase to $41,000 year, your annual net increase will not be $6,000 or $500 per month. It will only increase about $350 monthly or $4,200 a year. Taxes get the rest of your raise.

GUARD YOUR HEALTH

If paying your monthly health insurance premiums is too hard to do, what will happen if you have to go to the emergency room? A simple broken arm being cast in the local hospital can easily cost $5000. You need to have some kind of insurance that will assist with the big things. However, the best way to deal with an occasional visit to the doctor is with cash. And consider it a financial strategy: stay or get healthy. Stop smoking and excessive drinking. Stop eating at McDonalds and learn to like salads. You should also put down that cell phone when driving.

PERSONAL BUDGET

No successful business has ever operated without having a budget. It is simply impossible. Why should we think that our personal lives and home can operate with a budget? To not have a personal budget is simply illogical and is a plan for disaster. People who attempt to live and operate without some sort of budget and budget plan will fail financially. Period. Your personal budget is also a living creature. It will grow and evolve as your career and personal life grows and changes.

There are many types of budgeting systems, computer programs, applications, and a growing crowd of people who will assist you making a budget. However, the best and most effective personal budgets are those that you create for yourself. Do not ask, much less pay for someone to create a budget for you. Ask for help, but personal budgets are just that: they are personalized to each person or family.

You do not need to have an MBA to manage your personal finances. You do not have to have a fancy computer program. A pencil and paper will suffice. Add some envelopes to the pencil and paper and you have a great budgeting tool that is visible (thus making it a constant reminder of its purpose), easy to operate, and will also reward you for staying on budget. In fact let's look at the envelope system. And by the way, I began using this system in 1984 when I found myself in an early financial hole that I dug myself into due to a lack of discipline. It got me out of my hole.

THE ENVELOPE BUDGET SYSTEM

The envelope system has been around for many decades; it is not new. Rather it is a useful, simple tool.

It works because it provides physical characteristics to a budget. Using the envelope system allows you to see and to touch the money that is being spent and saved. These are undeniable reminders of what we are doing. The envelope system removes the abstractness of electronic money. And though it is a proven tool and has been in use for years, many people still have not heard of it or know if its usefulness or realize just how easy it is. So long as cash is still being accepted as payment in stores, the envelope system will work.

You can start the program today. You do not need to have already saved money to start using the envelope system.

First step, list all of your monthly expenses using the pencil and paper we talked about. Include ALL of your expenses. List them according to as many categories as you would like. I suggest being pretty detailed, but without going overboard. You will want to have at least the following categories if applicable:

- Rent
- Utilities
- Transportation (gasoline, bus, taxi, etc.)
- Car and insurance payments
- Loan payments
- Groceries
- Clothing
- Restaurant/date night

- Church/charity
- Emergency Fund (must have this category)

Try to use cash for all purchases, paying bills, etc. Using cash is a visual reminder of how and when we are giving away our money.

Now total up the amounts from the categories that you can pay for with cash. This will definitely include groceries, church/charity, clothing, and restaurant/date night. Get some envelopes and label one with each of the categories that you have listed. Also, write the monthly budget amount for each category on the envelope. Total up the amounts for all the categories that you can pay for with cash money; groceries, restaurants, emergency fund, clothing, and possibly transportation should be listed in this total. Include as many categories as possible. Convenience should not be an issue. Convenience costs money. Attempt to pay for things with cash so long as it does not cost more money to use cash! If it takes walking into the gas station to use cash, make the walk. And do not forget the emergency fund. You must put something into it with each paycheck. You decide what this should be by looking at your income and expenditures. This total of all the cash accounts will be your monthly cash allowance.

When you receive your monthly paycheck, write yourself a check for your monthly cash allowance. Ask for the cash in small bills. Do not get all big bills. The idea is that if you go the market to purchase a loaf of bread and only a loaf of bread, you can take only the amount needed for the purchase into the market with you. If the loaf of bread costs $1.90 then you take two $1 bills with you. You do not want to have too much money in hand when shopping or making purchases – no change back means that you cannot pick up that candy bar you really do not need.

Now, divide out the cash into the appropriate envelopes.

When it is time to make a purchase, take only money from the appropriate envelope to make the purchase. No money comes out of any other envelope except the designated envelope to make purchases for any reason. Take only enough money to cover the impending purchase. Do not take any more than necessary. If you need $5 worth of gasoline, take a $5 bill. Do not take a $10 bill. Any change goes back into that envelope. If at the grocery store and your budget for the week is $100 and you have $110 in the cart, trade items down for a less expensive brand or change your menu.

Get a receipt for every purchase you make. When using a credit card get a receipt. Get a receipt from gas pumps. Ask for the receipt for the drink and bag of nuts that you get while pumping the gasoline. If you do not get a receipt, make a note with the date, what you bought, and the amount. Receipts show us what our spending habits are and will show us those areas in which we can make changes in order to save money.

Put all receipts and notes into the appropriate envelopes.

For those categories that you must pay for with a credit card, you will need to have a piece of paper with the envelope or you can use the outside of the envelope. Subtract the amount of the purchase from the budget amount for that category. Keep a constant running balance of how much money is available to use for that category.

Do not cheat on the envelopes. Try not to borrow from envelopes. Rather, adjust your budget if you need to. Working budgets should only be adjusted when there is a proven need to. Budgets should not be changed on a whim or without good reason. If your restaurant envelope is empty do not take money from the clothing envelope. You will need the accumulated two months clothing money next month when you need to buy new shoes.

Next month, repeat the process, adding cash to the cash envelopes or adding the new budgeted amount to the non-cash envelopes.

Reward yourself. If there is some extra money in the restaurant envelope then use it for rewarding yourself. You might take some of that extra money and put it into a new envelope and label that envelope new car or vacation money. Rewarding yourself is important as that is what helps to motivate us in maintaining financial discipline. You can live on a bean-and-rice diet, but having a dessert every now and then is really nice.

The reason for the envelope system is to teach and to encourage discipline and to reduce unnecessary spending. If the grocery envelope is nearly empty, then you eat leftovers or you buy beans instead of steak. If the gasoline budget is almost gone, then you carpool or you do not take the trip to the beach.

If a crisis happens during the month then you talk to the spouse and the two of you figure out the best course of action. Only take money from the emergency fund if no other option is available. If might be better to eat beans and rice for the remainder of the month or to take a sandwich to work for a couple of weeks instead of eating out than it is to take from the emergency fund. Basically, your definition of emergency may need to change from uncomfortable or undesirable to something a bit more serious.

As powerful as the envelope system is for corralling your spending, it is not the most powerful. The most powerful weapon for having financial success is you, your discipline, and your knowledge.

...LIFE SKILLS FOR ANY SUCCESSFUL BUSINESS OR CAREER

What I refer to as life skills are those behaviors that are required for the responsible and efficient managing of our personal affairs. These skills are used to handle problems and questions that we commonly encounter in our daily human life. In particular, I am referring to those life skills that are needed for developing and managing and maintaining relationships. As relationships are vital for any successful business or organization, a successful business owner should strive to develop and use these life skills. The greatest part of your financial and social success in life is determined by your communication and social skills.

Our ability to assess and to monitor our own emotions (emotional intelligence) while assessing and monitoring the emotions of those around us and then to use that information to guide our actions and behaviors will produce much more success in our careers and lives than any amount of cognitive intelligence. Emotional intelligence is composed primarily of social competence. Many studies have indicated that people with high emotional intelligence have better mental health, greater job performance, and more compelling leadership skills.[11] Our success as adults depends upon the adult's foundation of social skills.

Every business involves people. Business is all about relationships within and connected to that business – relationships with customers, peers, bosses, employees,

---

[11]Barbey, Aron K.; Colom, Roberto; Grafman, Jordan. "Distributed neural system for emotional intelligence revealed by lesion mapping". *Social Cognitive and Affective Neuroscience* 9 (3): 265–272

and those who provide services to us. The quality of our work and the level of our business performance is directly affected by our relationships with the various people we connect with. Our relationships must be genuine. It is imperative to that we truly care about our colleagues. We must really want to know what their ideas are and how they feel about decisions to be made. We must be encouraging. We must want to help people to succeed as much as we want to succeed.

EMOTIONAL INTELLIGENCE

Unlike our intelligence quotient that remains more or less stable throughout our lifetime, our ability to learn about our emotions and the emotions of others is very flexible. And while our base personalities do not change that much after our early adolescent years – if I am in introvert at heart at age sixteen, I will probably forever be an introvert – I can learn to manage myself so that my bent as an introvert is not so overt. I can decide that when I enter a crowded room that I will start conversations. I can purpose myself to look people in the face when we are conversing. Yes, I may be out of my comfort level doing these things, however I do these things because I know that not only are my actions beneficial to me, but that these actions are beneficial to the other person. My conversation may be exactly what the other person might need to hear. The other person will realize that I consider him or her as important by my attentive listening.

There are four basic of emotional intelligence:

- **Self-awareness.** This is our capability to recognize our emotions and to sense when those emotions are affecting our behavior and actions. Self-awareness allows us to understand our bents and tendencies and why we act the way we do.
- **Social awareness.** This is our ability to recognize and to sense the emotions of others. We are able detect when and what emotions are affecting the behavior and actions of others. We pick up on what people are feeling and thinking. We suspect as to why they are feeling as they do and have an idea of what they may want or need.
- **Self-management.** This is our using the self-awareness of our emotions to adapt to situations. Self-management allows us to respond thoughtfully to events and revelations rather than simply reacting.
- **Relationship management.** This is the ability to use our awareness of emotions in ourselves and in those around us to better manage our relationships with those others to more successful, less problematic outcomes.

Emotional intelligence is and should be a major part of our daily lives not only in the workplace but also in the home and in our daily social lives. Emotional intelligence is our having empathy for others; an empathy that places ourselves in the place of another in order to have a sense of how they feel and perhaps even why they feel that way. Having emotional intelligence allows us to put others at ease, allows them to have confidence in us, and conveys the fact that we respect and care about them. Any relationship worth having is built upon respect and trust.

So why is emotional intelligence so important in business? Who would you rather do business with:

Someone who does an excellent job of taking care of your yard and flower gardens and landscaping work but acts disgruntled, upset, inattentive, and bothered by your suggesting something new or different

> *If all other factors are equal, the higher the social competence of an entrepreneur, the greater financial success of the entrepreneur.*

or

Someone who does a good job of taking care of your yard and flower gardens and landscaping work and is not only willing to but happy and excited to make changes and do something new and different in the yard and landscaping?

Someone who is pleasant to work with will is nearly always chosen over someone who might be a tad bit technically superior in the same task. The same concept works for employees. The better employees will choose to work for the more agreeable employers. Harvard Business School research has shown overwhelmingly that people would rather work with someone likeable and less skilled than with someone who is highly capable but disagreeable, impolite, or withdrawn.[12]

If all other factors are equal, the higher the social competence of an entrepreneur, the greater financial success of the entrepreneur.

...ETHICS, MORALS AND VALUES

What is the difference between ethics, morals and values?

There is not complete agreement among those people who attempt to answer this question. For some, the answer to this question is dependent upon the academic discipline that has shaped your thinking or the theological or religious basis of a personal belief system. Therefore, in answering this question, a question that seems as if it should be easy and simple to answer, it is necessary to explain even the simplest answer.

I am answering the question from a businessperson's perspective, though I must admit the philosopher and

---

[12] Trunk, Penelope. "Social Skills Matter More than Ever, so Here's How to Get Them." Penelope Trunk Careers. July 18, 2006. Accessed September 20, 2014.

theologian in me will probably have an appearance in my answer. Perhaps the answer will be a helpful compromise of the business person's utility and an academic's sophistication and rigor.

Now that I have leveraged my answer with a caveat, let's look at these three concepts, though in reverse order.

VALUES ARE OUR FUNDAMENTAL BELIEFS

Values are the doctrines we use to define right, good and just. Values offer guidance as we decide what is right and what is wrong. Values are our most basic standards.

Think of the word "evaluate". When evaluating something we are comparing it to a standard. We decide whether that something achieves that standard or if that something falls short. We observe whether that something comes close to or far exceeds the standard which it is being compared to.

Emblematic values include integrity, honesty, compassion, honor, courage, responsibility, respect, patriotism, and fairness.

MORALS ARE VALUES WHICH WE ASCRIBE TO A BELIEF SYSTEM

A belief system, typically a theological or religious system or political system, affect values to us. These directed values have authority due to something outside the individual. This something is a higher being or higher authority (i.e. society). In today's business world in many political environs, business owners and leaders often avoid framing ethical choice in terms of morality due to fear of offending someone with a different belief system. The business does not want to be perceived as lacking respect or compassion for different beliefs. But most of us do find our values greatly influenced by a sense of morality. This moral correctness as defined by a higher authority. We do not cite that authority because we do not desire to appear irrational, illogical, or emotionally reactive to those who do not share our belief system. However, this absence of public reference of our morals does not weaken the power of a moral authority. Sidestepping a morality-based rationale is a social convention; a social convention that is not widely practiced. Human nature allows for and desires a higher authority above the individual.

Using this definition for morals, we can label the above values as "moral values". They are values that are derived from a high authority. This separates them from business values such as quality, excellence, safety, and service. These are useful values and are considered right in a business context but would have different meanings as morals.

ETHICS REFERS TO OUR ACTIONS AND DECISIONS

Acting in ways that are consistent with our beliefs (from a secular belief system or from a moral authority) we characterize as ethical behavior. If we act in ways that are not parallel with our values that tell us what is right, good, and just, then we are acting unethically.

However, what is defined as ethical is not solely an individual exercise. If ethical behavior were left up only to the individual, it could be argued that Hitler's actions were ethical based upon his definition of right, good, and just. Whether or not our decisions and actions are ethical or unethical is defined by our societies and not by the individual.

Every day we find ethical dilemmas in the world around us. The dilemmas are not necessarily choices between what we think is wrong and what we think is right, but the most difficult dilemmas are between competing rights. Which is the higher right, that of the owner of a loaf of bread or that of the father who stole the loaf to feed his starving child?

ETHICS AND THE SMALL BUSINESS OWNER

Very few of us are business saints. All of us can probably look back and see some actions, events, and things we have done in business that we are not proud of. We have done some things that we may have thought were justified, but now wish we had not done. However, few of us are thieves.

Business ethics is a very large issue in today's society. With social media and the Internet, businesses must be more transparent. When perceived unethical behavior occurs, someone will find out.

Owners of small businesses owners must make ethical decision each day in the operating of their businesses. Sometimes these decisions involve customers and potential customers. Sometimes these decisions involve the administration of the business. However, both types of decisions can have severe impact upon the company's reputation and even financial situation in today's societies.

Making bad decisions that can be perceived as unethical will almost always begin small. "Let's delay paying the vendor for a week because we will need that cash for something else." Notice the word "because". We always have a justification for doing what we know is not right. While cash flow is a life and death issue for your business, it is also a life and death issue for most companies. Why do you think that the cash flow in your business is more important than the vendor's cash flow? What if all of the vendor's customers delayed a week to make payment past the due date? Did the vendor make a bad choice in taking you on as a customer?

Ethical problems in a business nearly always begin small. Many times we find ourselves out of bounds of our ethics because we made a series of snap decisions without thinking through the consequences of those decisions. But each small decision that you make creates the kind of businessperson that you are and will become. If you continually make unethical business decisions, you will be that unethical business person. Living and operating an ethical business is a continual effort.

IN CLOSING...

Everything comes back to one unavoidable principle and natural law of this universe:

You must spend less than you earn!

Multiple active income streams will help to ensure that your earnings are somewhat stable. They will help to close gaps between earnings and spending. However, minimizing spending is a better way in shrinking those gags. Make a serious commitment to spend less than you earn. Focus on paying down your debt with the difference in your earning and your spending once you have built a small emergency fund.

Next figure out what you are good at doing. When you know that, figure out a way to make some additional cash from what you are good at doing. There is usually a market of some sort for most our traits and skills.

Once you know what you are good at and know of a way to make some money, commit some time. Turn off the television for a couple of hours each day. Use that time to make some money with that new found time. Chances are good that you can make some cash, though maybe not much in the beginning, with your time. This time will become your first alternative income stream.

Then use the cash from that first income stream to something financially positive. Do not spend the money right away. Instead pay down some more debt or invest it into another income stream.

Our real goal should be financial independence. If we are not completely dependent upon one sole income stream – like a primary job – then we have some independence to have and to make more choices in our lives that will make our lives more enjoyable, rewarding, and meaningful.

ABOUT THE AUTHOR

The author is an entrepreneur that has owned and operated several businesses. He has also coached personnel in leadership roles in international corporations and organizations in Asia, and Middle East.

www.ingramcontent.com/pod-product-compliance
Lightning Source LLC
Chambersburg PA
CBHW061323220326
41599CB00026B/4998